The Art of Bliss

Tess Whitehurst is an intuitive counselor, energy worker, feng shui consultant, and speaker. She has appeared on the Bravo TV show *Flipping Out*, and her writing has been featured in such places as the AOL welcome page, Llewellyn's annuals, and the *Whole Life Times* blog. To learn about her workshops, writings, and appearances, and to sign up for her free monthly newsletter, visit her online:

www.tesswhitehurst.com

Finding Your Center,

Getting in the Flow

&

Creating the Life You Desire

The Art of Bliss

Tess Whitehurst

Llewellyn Publications
WOODBURY, MINNESOTA

FIRST EDITION
First Printing, 2012

Book design and edit by Rebecca Zins
Cover sea: iStockphoto.conm/BingoPixel
Cover design by Lisa Novak
Interior flower ornament from the Fleurons of Hope font
Interior floor plan illustrations by the Llewellyn Art Department

Llewellyn Publications is a registered trademark
of Llewellyn Worldwide Ltd.

Library of Congress Cataloging-in-Publication Data
Whitehurst, Tess, 1977–
 The art of bliss : finding your center, getting in the flow, and creating the life you desire / Tess Whitehurst.—1st ed.
     p. cm.
 Includes bibliographical references.
 ISBN 978-0-7387-3196-4
 1. Spiritual life. 2. Self-actualization (Psychology)—Religious aspects—Taoism. 3. Yi jing. I. Title.
 BL624.W477 2012
 158—dc23

2012017589

Llewellyn Publications
A Division of Llewellyn Worldwide Ltd.
2143 Wooddale Drive
Woodbury, MN 55125-2989

www.llewellyn.com

Printed in the United States of America

Contents

Introduction

I am so excited about this book!

Since authors do such things in introductions, let me begin by telling you about the events leading up to its birth.

About fourteen years ago, I had a really great translation of the I Ching. I have since lost it, and I can't remember which one it was, but I do remember the consistently clear and illuminating readings I experienced with it. At the time, I didn't know much about its origins (other than that Carl Jung liked it, which is why I picked up a copy), but I did know that I loved it. I had already been enthusiastically studying Wicca and natural magic, and I found that the I Ching helped me connect with the same type of energy I connected with during rituals—in essence, the divine energy that inspired me, uplifted me, united me with my intuition and guidance, and allowed me to consciously shift my life conditions for the better.

Five years later, I became interested in feng shui and attended the Western School of Feng Shui in San Diego.

Once again, the eight trigrams—the three-line symbols that create the backbone of the I Ching—appeared, this time imbedded within the hexagrams (the six-line symbols, or groupings of two trigrams) that make up the feng shui floor plan, or bagua. After learning about each life area and how it was associated with an element of nature as denoted in the I Ching (which I now knew was perhaps the oldest of all known books and the backbone of Chinese philosophy), I began to recognize the spiraling interplay of these same energies in the physical world, and I began to realize that these visible manifestations were connected to the invisible dynamics at work in my (and everyone's) life.

This realization was life altering. Before the realization, I had a sort of free-floating anxiety that felt like I was driving a car but couldn't see out the windshield. After the realization—when I saw that everything going on in my internal world affects everything in my external world (and vice versa), and when I had tools that could help me understand and work with this connection in a powerful way—I felt so much safer and more grounded. Now these two formerly disparate aspects of life—seen and unseen, known and unknown, fleeting and eternal—were united in my consciousness. And this felt truer, more real, and infinitely more empowering.

The more I worked with the nine areas of the bagua (or feng shui floor plan), the more I came to recognize them as far more than just simple areas of the home or answers in an I Ching reading. I saw very clearly that they comprise nine life keys that we can consciously activate and balance in order to bring harmony and success into every area of our lives. And perhaps the most exciting thing of all is that there is no end to the wisdom that they contain. The wisdom spirals endlessly and appears in an infinite number of facets and variations, not just in our homes, but also in our minds, bodies, emotions, and life conditions. What's more, these keys are not exclusive to any one culture or tradition. Once you learn to recognize their energy, you will see that they are universal energies that can correspond with any spiritual system, healing modality, or cosmology.

Still, as a feng shui consultant and teacher, and later as a metaphysical author and lecturer, I soon learned that, while most people deeply crave the wisdom behind these nine life keys, the depth of it was often lost in the translation. In my consultations and lectures, although I often got carried away discussing the dynamics and nuances of this wisdom, I felt that I only had the time to barely scratch the surface—to give some general information but not to teach these keys as the kaleidoscopic, scintillating language of the spirit that they really are. In other words, while I so desperately wanted to share the gift of this way of seeing and interacting with the world, I could only go so far.

Which brings me to why I am so excited about this book. It is designed so that you will not just read about the nine life keys, but you will also experience them: recognize them in your life, see them visibly at work in your home and in the natural world, learn how each key interacts with each other key, and consciously work with them to create lasting and satisfying positive change in your life. And believe me, your life will never be the same. You, too, will finally be able to see through the windshield to infinity while you maneuver the temporal vehicle that is your current life experience. As you observe that you reside in both worlds simultaneously (infinite and temporal/heaven and earth), you will find that you always have the power to change your outlook and your life conditions for the better, no matter what. You will also find that the wisdom of the nine life keys will endlessly gain depth and dimension as you progress through life, spiraling you deeper and deeper into the heart of the mystery and into bliss.

> I suddenly realized that in the language, or at any rate in the spirit of the Glass Bead Game, everything actually was all-meaningful, that every symbol and combination of symbols led not hither and yon, not to single examples, experiments, and proofs, but into the center, the mystery and innermost heart of the world, into primal knowledge. Every transition from major to minor in a sonata, every transformation of a myth or a religious cult, every classical or artistic formulation was, I realized in that flashing moment, if seen with truly a meditative mind, nothing but a direct route into the interior of the cosmic mystery, where in the alternation between inhaling and exhaling, between heaven and earth, between Yin and Yang, holiness is forever being created.
>
> Hermann Hesse,
> *Magister Ludi (The Glass Bead Game)*

Read This First

To orient you to the wisdom contained in this book, I ask you to consider a dream. No matter how scary or unsettling the dream may be, the entire time you're having it, you're lying comfortably in your bed, safe and sound, in a state of total relaxation and almost complete stillness. All of the nonsensical drama of the dream—even if it seems to span months, years, or lifetimes—is only hours, minutes, or seconds away from resolving itself completely by evaporating into the ethers of oblivion and returning to the total nonreality from which it came.

The observer in your mind—your conscious awareness—traverses dreams and waking life in the same way, and neither seems to have rhyme or reason. Neither seems to make sense. But beneath the movement, drama, and seeming discord, there is a quiet stillness that allows and contains and watches without judging. It's like the open space of sky in which the clouds appear and shift and change and then dissolve. Because it's so free of conflict and so one with everything, we might call this stillness bliss.

It's said that those who have the best and most enjoyable dreams are those who are consciously aware of this bliss: they are in touch with the observer behind it all. In other words, they know that it is all a dream. As you're probably aware, this kind of dreaming is called lucid dreaming. Interestingly, when we're engaged in lucid dreaming, we're empowered to intentionally affect the story of our dream and manifest the conditions that we would most like to experience.

Even more interestingly, the same mechanism applies to waking life.

True, in waking life we are bound by certain natural laws that don't seem to matter much when we are dreaming. We can't simply grow wings and fly away, for example. And, also unlike when we are dreaming, our manifestations might not all be instantaneous. But when we accept the limitations of time and space that seem to characterize this particular (waking) dream, we can work *with* them rather than against them. In fact, we can even use the appearance of limitation as a magical tool: like a single solar panel soaking up the unlimited power of the sun to light up a room, the "limited" conditions in this plane of existence can allow bliss to shine forth and run like a current of energy through every area of our life experience.

What You're About to Learn

You're about to learn a magical and spiritual system that will allow you to rediscover and reconnect with the bliss that is your natural state. Once you reconnect with the bliss, you will become aware that it is not only an inner state, but it is also an energy that animates and underlies your life conditions and, in fact, everything that you are and everything that you perceive. You will then become empowered to channel this energy into creating enjoyable and satisfying life conditions.

In feng shui, this energy is called chi. In yoga, it's called prana. In ancient Egypt, it was called heka. It might be defined as a "divine life force," as it's the energy from which everything is made and to which everything returns. For our purposes, we'll call it bliss.

Imagine that bliss is water and that you are a river. Whether you're conscious of it or not, you're a vessel through which bliss temporarily flows. As such, you have a particular nature: the bliss flows through you in a certain direction and according to certain natural laws.

The idea is that we will have the most success in all life areas when we are flowing with bliss (which we are a part of) rather than attempting to flow against it or in a different direction altogether. This might be an aspect of what Joseph Campbell meant when he said, "Follow your bliss."

But to follow our bliss, we must first *connect* with our bliss. Then we realize that we *are* our bliss and that everything else is an illusion. The illusion may not go away, but when we know that it's an illusion, we are free to traverse it in much the same way that a lucid dreamer traverses a dream.

This means that we can:

- Make the breakthroughs we've been wanting to make

- Discover our most ideal career and life path

- Establish and maintain positive self-care habits

- Enhance our physical health

- Open ourselves up to receive prosperity and blessings of all forms

- Feel confident sharing our gifts and shining our light in the world

- Experience the kind of romance we want

- Express our creativity in satisfying ways

- Experience synchronicity and
  flow in all life areas

- Experience true self-love

- Heal our relationships with others

- Experience inner balance and equilibrium

- Heal and empower ourselves in
  precisely the way our soul craves

- Create the conditions we desire

This does not mean that we no longer encounter challenges. What it does mean is we take responsibility for our lives. In other words, we gratefully learn from every experience, and we're empowered to first accept and then lovingly shift what we don't like rather than feel hopeless or victimized. It also means that we align with an internal compass that helps us stay true to our most ideal life flow.

How to Read This Book

While you can, of course, read this book in any way that feels right to you, I suggest that you casually read it all the way through once to get oriented to its teachings, then read it again more carefully, taking time with it and performing the exercises and rituals that call to you.

Essential Ancient Secrets

There are two magical secrets that we must touch on before we proceed, both of which make up the backbone of this book. The first is an ancient mathematical construct; the second is an omnipresent spiritual concept. Both of these secrets appear in a number of cultures and cosmologies. Perhaps more importantly, both of these secrets are highly effective methods of consciously uniting the seen and unseen worlds for the purpose of connecting with the Infinite and consciously effecting positive change—and this is the essence of the alchemy of bliss.

ANCIENT SECRET #1

In the Taoist form of alchemy that we call feng shui, there is a mathematical and magical construct known as the bagua. In Western mystery traditions it's known as a magic square (a square in which each row adds up to the same number) or, more specifically, as the square of Saturn. In fact, the bagua/square of Saturn is present in some form in the mathematical and spiritual traditions of countless cultures, both Western and Eastern. It looks like a tick-tack-toe board in which each square contains a number. If you take a moment to investigate, you'll notice that each row on the board, whether horizontal, vertical, or diagonal, adds up to the number fifteen.

4	9	2
3	5	7
8	1	6

In feng shui, each square in the bagua corresponds with an aspect, or hexagram (six-line symbol made up of two three-line symbols put together), of the I Ching, the most ancient known book and divination system. Each hexagram and square also corresponds with an aspect of nature and a major life area. For example, the square in the middle of the bottom row (1) corresponds with deep water as well as with one's career and most ideal life path. (Please note that while each square is energetically aligned with the number that appears in the diagram above, for the sake of clarity and continuity, the chapters and corresponding life keys are numbered differently in this book.)

Western magical traditions associate this particular magic square with the planet Saturn: the planet of earthiness and limitation. This is notable because the bagua, or square of Saturn, is an alchemical map that works within the *appearance* of limitation to help us find our way back to a connection with the infinite bliss that is our natural state.

To illustrate this, imagine sunlight streaming through a clear prism or wind blowing through melodious chimes.

The sunlight is sunlight, and the wind is wind. Still, by flowing through something that appears limited (the prism or chimes), the sunlight creates rainbows, just as the wind rings the chimes. Similarly, an infinite life force flows through our present finite "reality" (our existence and perceptions) to create the holographic interplay of stories that we call our life conditions. The bagua/square of Saturn is a symbol, or conceptual construct, of that mechanism. It gives us a framework and reference point for effecting positive change through working between the realms of finite and infinite, seen and unseen, form and spirit.

As you will see, by calibrating the nine life areas that make up the bagua, we calibrate our lives and become free to perceive and dance with the current of bliss that flows through everything.

ANCIENT SECRET #2

In perhaps every ancient culture, there have been altars. An altar is a spiritual focal point that connects our spiritual inspiration with the physical world. It makes the invisible visible, and through its visibility it helps guide and influence divine, invisible life-force energy (bliss).

An altar might be as simple as a single statue on a shelf, or it might be as elaborate as a dining room table filled with framed pictures, candles, food, Christmas lights, flowers, and dozens of other things. As long as we know what we want it to represent and the energies we'd like it to hold and summon, and as long as it successfully embodies and enhances our divine inspiration, it's an altar.

By this definition, and provided it is truly inspired and thoughtfully placed, every charm, work of art, flower arrangement, and significant assemblage of objects may be perceived as an altar in itself.

Reasons for designating altars may include:

- To honor or request help from a specific deity or deities
- To manifest an intention, such as to increase abundance or draw in a new love interest
- To express our love toward and connect with our deceased loved ones
- To increase the sweetness and harmony in a household
- To enhance any life area in any way

Traditionally, altars are created on flat surfaces such as a small table, a shelf, or the top of a dresser. They usually have a focal point such as a picture of a divinity or something that represents the intention the altar is made to represent. Then they're often decorated with a candle or two, incense, and other objects such as flowers or fruit. But, in truth, there is no limit to what can and can't go on an altar. In fact, an altar can even be a single object such as a statue or a crystal, one or more framed pictures on the wall, a corner of the garden, a potted plant, or even a consciously chosen and assembled collection of magnets on the refrigerator.

When you go beyond duality and see inner and outer as inextricably connected and constantly dancing with and influencing one another, you can see that every area of your home has the potential to be perceived as its own altar. And when we interact with our entire home as if it were a living, breathing, multifaceted altar, our life conditions become united with the Divine, and our everyday existence becomes a portal into the sublime.

Prerequisites

There are three prerequisites that will allow you to receive maximum benefits from the teachings in the following chapters. Not only that, but each is a powerful magical exercise in its own right.

ALCHEMICAL PREREQUISITE #1

The first is this: clear your clutter. All of it! From everywhere! (Or at least get a pretty good head start.) If you don't love it, don't use it, or don't need it, *get rid of it.*

Why? Because everything is connected. Clutter in our home, car, desk, and storage space equals clutter in our mind, body, emotions, and life conditions. Simply put, clutter holds us back and blocks the natural flow of our bliss.

As simple and commonplace as it may seem, clearing clutter can move you further toward opening the way for bliss in your life than any other single recommendation in this book.

To give you an idea of the types of things that may constitute clutter, here's a clutter-clearing checklist (from my first book, *Magical Housekeeping: Simple Charms and Practical Tips for Creating a Harmonious Home*):

Paper

- Old receipts
- Old warranties and other unnecessary documents
- Junk mail
- Old cards and love letters
- Expired coupons

Clothes

- Clothes that don't fit
- Clothes you don't love
- Clothes that make you feel unattractive or less than stunning
- Clothes you never wear
- Clothes needing repair that you know you'll never repair

Books

- Any book you'll never open again

Decorations

- Any decoration that doesn't uplift you or bring you joy
- Any image depicting a condition or feeling you don't want to experience
- Dried or faux flowers or plants that appear faded, dusty, brittle, or overly dead

Furniture

- Any piece that doesn't fit in your space
- Any bed, couch, or dining table you shared with an ex-partner
- Anything you don't love
- Pieces that injure, trip, or inconvenience you

Gifts

- Anything you're hanging on to out of guilt or obligation

Food

- Anything you're honestly never going to eat

Car Clutter

- Trash
- Anything that doesn't belong in your car

Unfinished Projects

- Anything you're not going to (honestly) finish in the next month

Broken Things

- Any broken item you can't or aren't willing to fix (unless it's still useful and convenient and you honestly don't mind that it's a little bit broken)

Items with Negative Associations

- Gifts or hand-me-downs from people with whom you have negative associations
- Anything that reminds you of a negative situation or period

Take as long as you need with this clutter-clearing process. If you feel overwhelmed and you don't know where to start, choose one baby step that you feel comfortable with, such as clearing out a single drawer. Then clear out that drawer. Usually, that will spark your interest and gather momentum, but if it doesn't, just repeat the baby-step process as often as possible until your clutter-clearing engine is revved. (You might also check out my first book, *Magical Housekeeping*, or my ebook, *Magical Clutter Clearing Boot Camp*.)

ALCHEMICAL PREREQUISITE #2

Next, if you don't already have one lying around somewhere, you're going to have to compose a very simple drawing of the floor plan of your home. Believe me: it's really not as hard as it may sound! It just entails a tape measure (just to get it as close to scale as possible), a piece of graph paper, and a tiny bit of patient determination. And keep it simple: all you need to draw are the walls, doors, and perimeter of the space. (No need to worry about things like windows, toilets, or drawing the burners on the stove!) Again, there's no need to go crazy: just get it as close to scale as possible so that you have a good working idea of the layout of your home.

Here are a few additional tips:

- Include any attached garages or attached covered patios. (If they're not attached or covered, leave them out. The one exception would be if it were a raised patio that is contained by railings: if it is attached to the home, even if it is not covered, include it.)

- If you live in an apartment, just include the boundaries of your personal space. Include attached balconies or attached covered patios.

- If you rent a room or live with parents or roommates, just include the room that is uniquely yours.

ALCHEMICAL PREREQUISITE #3

As the final prerequisite, draw the square of Saturn over your floor plan. To do this, follow these simple steps:

1. If the outside border of your floor plan is not already a perfect square or rectangle, make it into one by extending the sides in order to complete any "missing areas." (See dark dotted lines on top figure of page 18.)

2. Draw an arrow at the front door/main entrance (as intended by the architect, even if you use another one more often) that's pointing in toward the home.

3. If necessary, rotate the paper so that the arrow is pointing up.

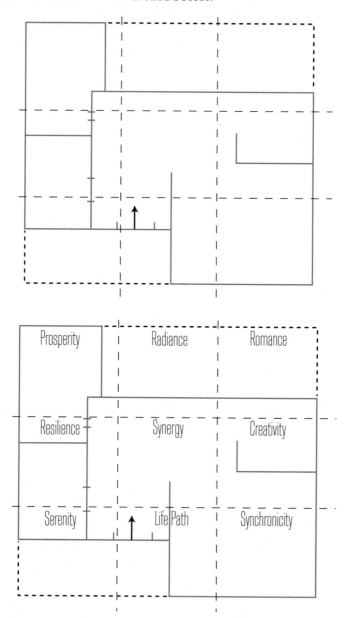

4. Draw a tick-tack-toe board over the square/ rectangle, dividing the floor plan into nine equal parts. (See top figure on opposite page.)

5. In the upper left corner, write the word *prosperity*. In the top middle, write the word *radiance*. In the top right, write the word *romance*. In the middle row on the far left, write the word *resilience*. In the very center, write the word *synergy*. In the middle row on the far right, write the word *creativity*. In the lower left-hand corner, write the word *serenity*. In the lower row in the middle, write the words *life path*. In the lower right-hand corner, write the word *synchronicity*.

As you'll discover in chapter 1, this drawing will come in handy, because one of the ways we unite the teachings of the bagua/square of Saturn with our lives is by recognizing them within the boundaries of our homes so that we can place herbs, crystals, and visual representations of our intentions accordingly.

Please note: for additional floors, the floor plan extends straight up or down from the floor containing the front door. In other words, if it's directly above (or below) the prosperity area, it's also the prosperity area.

Also note: if one or more areas lie outside your floor plan, see the appendix.

A Few More Considerations

You may have gleaned by now that there are nine life keys (or life areas) that make up the teachings in this book, each of which corresponds with one of the eight trigrams of the I Ching (or, in the case of the ninth key, the absence of a trigram). Immediately following this chapter, you'll find that each key is presented in a single chapter, which begins by orienting you to the key, moves on to magical symbols and practices that can help you to heal and align with the key, and concludes with a master ritual to help you activate the key in a clear and definite way.

I suggest that you use the first part of each chapter to subtly begin to align yourself with its energy, and as a diagnostic tool to tune in to how this key is already flowing in your life. Then, in the alchemy section, select the symbols and exercises that you intuitively feel will help balance and heal this key for you in the most ideal ways. *There is no need to do every exercise or employ every suggestion.* In fact, after reading through the chapter, if you feel that the key is already flowing for you in a relatively positive way, you might want to move ahead to the next key so that you can concentrate first on the key that feels the most crucial to you at this particular time in your life.

Remember that the art of bliss is ongoing. In other words, do not expect or aim to reach a point at which you and everything in your life fall into an inert state of perfection. As long as we are alive, we are changing and growing and evolving, and our spiritual/magical practice is intended to be a constant companion and support system throughout these ever-present shifts.

Also remember that the art of bliss is a holistic science. In other words, each key affects and interacts with each other key. The aim is balance and activation of all nine keys so that each one can thrive, so that you can enjoy success and happiness in all life areas, and so that simply by existing, you can be a beacon of healing and positivity for other people and the planet.

1 | Serenity

Envision a tall mountain in a remote natural setting. The sky is a brilliant blue, and the air is crisp and clean. There is a very light breeze, and bright greenery grows abundantly in every direction. The mountain is vast, ancient, and eminently still. As you gaze at it, you realize that while you are grounded in a deep sense of inner calm, you also feel exhilarated, inspired, motivated, and vitally interested in your own life experience.

**This is the alchemical essence
of life key #1: serenity.**

If the energies associated with this life key are flowing harmoniously, the following statements will be true for you (and the more ideal the flow, the truer they will be):

- Almost always, no matter how stressful things may appear or how stressed out I may seem to be on the outside, I feel I'm in touch with an inner sense of stillness and calm.

- I take at least a little bit of time almost every day to meditate or pray in peaceful solitude.

- I feel good about my exercise habits, and I exercise regularly.

- I actively pursue my interests and hobbies.

- I enjoy spending time outdoors in nature and make a point of doing so regularly.

- Most days, I think highly of myself, speak kindly to myself, and treat myself well.

- I enjoy learning new things, and I voluntarily take steps to deepen my knowledge and expertise in the areas that interest me.

- In general, I am filled with enthusiasm and vitality.

- I understand that good things can take time to build, and I feel comfortable with taking one step at a time and systematically moving toward my desires and dreams.

- I sleep deeply and get a good night's sleep most nights.

- I am respected and treated well by the people in my life.

- I am good at setting boundaries and saying no to things that don't feel right to me or that I can't comfortably fit into my schedule.

Qualities Associated with the Serenity Key

The following descriptions are designed to help you determine how well the serenity key is already flowing in your life and also to begin creating subtle shifts that will prepare you to more fully activate it. As you read, be sure not to judge or berate yourself if these qualities don't perfectly match your current life experience. Instead, relax, perform any or all of the suggested exercises (as you feel moved), and allow the descriptions to infuse your awareness with the qualities they represent.

STILLNESS

Behind all the seeming hustle and bustle taking place in your consciousness—the activities, obligations, conversations, thoughts, breaking news stories, emotions, etc.—there is a stillness. There is an alert, conscious awareness that is completely beyond time and all the chaotic happenings that appear to take place in time. There is an eternal, quiet, serene sense of calm.

This is true whether you realize it or not.

But when the serenity key is activated and flowing in your life, you do realize it. On some level, you're in touch with the empty space and silence that surround and underscore everything. Even when you're experiencing negative emotions such as fear or anger, there is an awareness of this quiet stillness somewhere in your consciousness, and it helps you keep things in perspective. It allows you the freedom to experience life without getting carried away in the drama and seeming discord of it all.

SOLITUDE

This world is a relentless mystery, and so is our existence. Where did we come from? Why are we here? What happens after we die? If we're not comfortable with these mysteries, spending time in quiet solitude can be something we loathe and try to avoid at all costs. When faced with it, we immediately turn on the television, text a friend, or invite someone over for drinks. But when we embrace these mysteries and allow them to infuse us with a sense of adventure and awe, quiet solitude can be something we revel in and happily anticipate.

Additionally, if we don't love, like, or think highly of ourselves, spending time with ourselves can feel just as bad as an abusive relationship or an awkward blind date.

Experiencing quiet solitude on a regular basis is a necessity when it comes to true harmony and joy, so it is both an act of self-love and—because it allows us to get to know ourselves better—an act which deepens our self-love.

Which brings us to…

SELF–LOVE

As the author Louise Hay says, "When we really love ourselves, everything in our life works." And love is infinite. So no matter how much you love yourself, you can always love yourself more. But how do we engender self-love? By speaking to ourselves kindly and gently, as we would to a child or a beloved friend, and by giving ourselves the gift of compassionate self-care, which includes exercise, good sleep, attractive clothes that we feel good in, time to relax and express our creativity, and more. Later in this chapter, you'll find rituals that can assist you in fostering self-love and fully activating the serenity key. You might also try any or all of the following self-love enhancement exercises.

Practice: REFLECTION OF LOVE

Light a candle (and perhaps light a stick of incense or diffuse lavender, ylang ylang, or another type of aromatherapeutic essential oil), relax, and gaze into your eyes in a mirror. Say lovely things to yourself. You might simply say "I love you." If you haven't been treating yourself well, you might say "I'm sorry." Speak from your heart and allow your emotions to flow as you reconnect with yourself in a tender and authentic way.

Practice: TOUCH OF LOVE

If you feel uneasiness in the pit of your stomach, grief in your heart, cramps in your uterus, or some other kind of physically located discomfort, place a hand or two over the ache and consciously send the energy of love to the part of your body that seems to be in distress. You might think about how grateful you are for that area of your body and marvel at its innate intelligence to perform its function in such an efficient and precise way, or you might simply conjure up a feeling of love and compassion in your heart and energetically direct it toward the area.

Or, as you lie in bed at night, you might send love to your stomach or heart (two important emotional centers) even if neither appears to be in any sort of distress at all, simply for the sake of increasing your self-love quotient.

Practice: BREATH OF LOVE

As you breathe in, realize that you are giving yourself the gift of nourishment. As you breathe out, realize that you are giving yourself the gift of cleansing and release. Bestow gift after gift after gift, and allow yourself to receive these gifts and be grateful for them.

This is a good one to do while you're in a waiting room, walking in nature, or relaxing in quiet solitude.

Practice: WORDS OF LOVE

Author Louise Hay recommends the affirmation "I love and approve of myself." I like to add this: "I am safe, and all is well." Whenever you feel that your mind is racing with thoughts that are not self-loving, try inwardly repeating: "I love and approve of myself. I am safe, and all is well." If you notice that your mind has begun to wander back to the stream of unloving thoughts, don't judge or berate yourself in the least! Simply smile tenderly toward yourself and return to the affirmation.

Practice: WATERS OF LOVE

Before you drink your water, bless it. Hold it in both hands and envision that it's filled with and emanating blindingly bright golden-white light like the sun. Think the words *self-love* and intuitively send the energy of the words into the water. (You can also send other words into the water as desired: *prosperity, happiness, success,* etc.)

PRAYER OR MEDITATION

There's a reason why spiritual teachers recommend that we spend at least a little bit of time in silent prayer or meditation daily. Both practices connect us with our divine source and infinite nature, and even as few as ten minutes a day engaged in either or both will positively affect every other moment of our day, whether we're awake or asleep.

STUDY

Learning is a form of self-cultivation and self-nourishment. Rather than studying for the sake of studying, or studying things that we couldn't care less about, it's important that we study what interests us and brings us joy, as our joy and interest are guideposts on the path to our most ideal life flow. (Still, if you hate calculus, and your heart of hearts wants to get a degree in something for which you need to take a calculus class, biting the bullet and passing the class can also be a form of self-nourishment.)

Listening to the curiosities and yearnings of your heart might lead you to anything from juggling to Asian history to exotic dance to brain surgery.

Journaling Exercise: LEARNING YOUR PASSIONS

This fun journaling exercise will help you to know yourself better and to get even clearer on your unique passions.

Make a list of the numbers 1 through 20. Take a few breaths and get into a relaxed and receptive state. Above the numbers, write: "If I had all the time and opportunities in the world, I'd learn _____." Then fill in the blank twenty times without censoring yourself or giving yourself time to talk yourself out of anything. You might even write whimsical answers, like "how to fly without an airplane" or "time travel." Upon later reflection, these answers might indicate that you'd like to scuba dive, hang glide, write sci-fi stories, or study theoretical physics.

EXERCISE

Exercising regularly (and enjoying it!) is another indication that you've got it going on in the serenity key department. Although exercise often gets a bad rap as being grueling, boring, or just plain unpleasant, once we get in the habit and find techniques that work for us, exercise really can become not just bearable, but one of the highlights of the day. Not only that, but the positive effects it has on our health, longevity, personal power, and state of mind are more than worth the extra effort. It's simply a matter of finding the right methods and establishing the right momentum.

Journaling Exercise: FINDING YOUR MOMENTUM

If you need to lay a little groundwork when it comes to getting in the exercise habit, try this.

In your journal or notebook, respond to the following:

1. On a scale of 1–5 (5 meaning "very difficult" and 1 meaning "very easy"), rate the following activities if you were to do them at this very moment:

   • Putting on some exercise clothes

- Walking slowly or stretching
  gently for five minutes

- Dancing in a leisurely way to a song
  that you like from beginning to end

2. Number 1–5. List five exercise-related
   activities that seem relatively doable to you
   (dancing, walking, yoga, basketball, etc.).

3. Number 1-5. List five sports or exercise-related
   activities that you've enjoyed in the past, that
   you've wanted to try, or that you like to watch.

4. On any given day, how much time do you
   spend doing the following activities:

   - Watching TV

   - Reading recreationally

   - Talking to friends on the phone or texting

   - Emailing, social networking,
     or surfing the Internet

5. Realistically, on any given day, do you
   feel that you could spare ten to twenty
   minutes from any of the above activities
   to spend on something else?

6. Number 1–10. Above the numbers, write: "In
   the past, I've known that I should exercise
   regularly, but I haven't because _____."
   Then—*without insulting or berating yourself*—
   fill in the blank ten times. (You might write:

"It seemed like too much work," "I felt
like I didn't have enough time," etc.)

7. Number 1-10. Above the numbers,
write: "If I exercised regularly, it would
be wonderful because _____."
Then fill in the blank ten times.

8. Compare your responses to numbers 6
and 7. Ultimately (according to your own
answers), which seems like the easier and more
enjoyable path: not exercising or exercising?

9. While considering your answers to the above
questions, write down one or two exercise-
related activities you might be willing to
commit to doing 3–5 times per week. (No
pressure: we are speaking hypothetically here.)
Even if it's just putting on your exercise clothes
and not lifting a finger other than that, or even
if it's just dancing to a three- or four-minute
song, that's okay. Something is always better
than nothing, and a huge momentum often
starts with the tiniest push (just ask a snowball).
In other words, you can always build up your
exercise practice little by little over time.

BOUNDARIES

Within each of us is a personal truth. This truth knows
unequivocally what feels right/what doesn't feel right, what's
okay with us/what's not okay with us, who we want to spend

time with/who we want to stay away from, when we want
to stay/when we want to leave, and what we want to say
yes to/what we want to say no to. Having good boundaries
means we are tapped into this truth: we know what it is, we
are comfortable speaking it aloud, and we make sure that we
honor it in all our relationships and in every situation.

SLEEP

When all of the qualities associated with this key are powerfully present in our lives (exercise, good boundaries, inner
stillness, self-love, etc.), a natural consequence is that we get
a good night's sleep almost every night. And the converse is
also true: a good night's sleep supports the qualities that are
associated with this key. This means that our sleep patterns
can be a good indication of the degree to which the serenity
key is flowing.

Here are some ideas for how to help yourself get a good
night's sleep:

- Exercise daily or almost daily.

- Make sure your bedroom is free of clutter
  and of items that remind you of activity
  (such as work items or exercise equipment).

- Make sure your bed is comfortable.

- Go light on caffeine and other stimulants,
  at least during the second half of the day.

- Eat lightly or not at all for at
  least two hours before bed.

- Try covering or removing bedroom mirrors (they contain a lot of energy and movement, and can sometimes keep us up).

- Place an amethyst near the head of your bed (see page 45).

- Cover bedroom windows in a way that helps you feel safe and secure.

SELF-CARE

Just as spending a day at the spa can help us relax, honor our body, and get back in touch with ourselves, attentive self-care is a self-nourishing and self-loving enterprise. Every time we shower, bathe, apply lotion, brush our teeth, condition our hair, or engage in any other regular self-care ritual, we have the opportunity to do it consciously and with great love. In this way we both exemplify and activate the serenity key.

TIME IN NATURE

Nature is the great healer. Spending quality time in nature tunes us right in to the divine flow like nothing else can. When the serenity key is flowing, we innately make time to spend time in nature on a regular basis. Conversely, when we make a point of spending time in nature on a regular basis, the serenity key usually becomes powerfully activated in our lives.

Serenity Key-Related Situations

Life situations and intentions that are related to the serenity key include:

- Feeling calm at your core in the midst of your day-to-day activities
- Experiencing grace under pressure
- Investing quality time in meditation and exercise
- Studying and taking tests
- Learning new skills of any kind
- Trips to the spa and self-care in general
- Enjoying quiet time in nature

Serenity Key Affirmations

I love and approve of myself.

I feel beautiful, and I am beautiful.

I enjoy taking care of myself.

There is a calm stillness residing at the core of my being.

I am enthusiastic and vitally interested in life.

I pursue my passions with enthusiasm.

It is safe for me to respect my own boundaries.

I stand in my power and honor my inner truth.

The Alchemy of Serenity

As above, so below. Visible mirrors invisible, and invisible mirrors visible. In truth, there is no duality. Everything is one with everything else, and inner and outer are one and the same. Knowing this, alchemists breathe life into the conditions we desire by clearly envisioning and believing in them while taking tangible, symbolic, intention-infused action in the physical world.

This is the first of many chapters that will invite you to put this concept into practice and to experience the magic for yourself.

Serenity Key Symbols

THE NUMBER EIGHT

Eight symbolizes eternity, infinity, and inner abundance: the space beyond time, where all things are possible and where you know that you are already in possession of everything you could ever want or need. Being truly in touch with these qualities—and allowing them to underscore your life experience—is the definition of serenity.

Here are some ideas for activating the serenity key with the number eight:

- Play relaxing and uplifting instrumental music with soft drums that beat in time to an eight-count beat as you clean house, meditate, read, drive, exercise, or work. (Or play it yourself if you're a musician.)

- Create or commission a serene piece of artwork depicting the number eight. Display it in the serenity area of your home, and empower it by standing near it, focusing on it, holding your hands in prayer pose, and repeating one of the serenity key affirmations nine times.

- Create a necklace with eight equally sized beads made of a crystal associated with the serenity key (see page 45). Place it in very bright sunlight for 5–10 minutes and then the light of a full moon for 20–40 minutes. Hold it in both hands and mentally direct the energy of one of the serenity key affirmations into the beads. Then wear it.

- Dissolve eight tablespoons of sea salt into a warm bath in a candlelit bathroom. Think the word *serenity* and mentally direct it into the water in the form of very bright blue light before soaking.

MOUNTAINS

The mountain is a classic symbol depicting the energy of this life key.

Here are some ideas for activating the serenity key with them:

- Go for a hike in the mountains.
- Go on a relaxing retreat in the mountains.

- Place mountain imagery in the
  serenity area of your home.

- As you meditate, sit with your spine straight
  and visualize/imagine/feel that you are a
  mountain. Then, imagine the mountain slowly
  getting smaller and smaller and more and more
  energetically potent until it resides in your
  heart or at the base of your spine, constantly
  infusing you with peace and calm. As you go
  through your daily activities, take a deep breath
  and get in touch with your inner mountain
  whenever your sense of serenity needs a boost.

SERENE NATURAL SETTINGS

Any beautiful natural setting where you can stand outside
on the earth can quickly and thoroughly infuse you with the
energies associated with the serenity key. This includes seascapes, forests, rivers, deserts, waterfalls, etc.

Here are some ideas for activating the serenity key with
them:

- Go camping.

- Go for a walk or a hike.

- Visit a lake or a beach.

- Place serene nature imagery in the
  serenity area of your home.

- Create a nature altar in the serenity area of
  your home. This might be a small table or shelf

devoted to items such as pine cones, rocks,
fresh wildflowers, naturally shed feathers, etc.

PLANTS, FLOWERS, AND TREES

Plants, flowers, and trees remind us of the fact that we are constantly learning and growing, and they can help us quiet our minds and tune in to the sublime subtlety of the spiritual realm.

Here are some ideas for activating the serenity key with them:

- Sit under a tree (even if it's just in your back yard).

- Hug a tree.

- Have a conversation with a plant, flower, tree, or rock by relaxing and silently tuning in.

- Bring healthy plants into your home.

- Work in your garden.

ROCKS

Like mountains, rocks are potent representations of equanimity, solidity, and stillness. What's more, each type of rock emits a healing vibration that can bring us into alignment with specific beneficial energies.

Here are some ideas for activating the serenity key with them:

- Work with crystals for healing purposes (see page 45 for ideas).

- Place a large rock or a healing crystal in the serenity area of your home.

Serenity Key Deities

Divinities that are associated with meditation, solitude, learning, wisdom, self-love, self-cultivation, and self-empowerment share the qualities and energy of the serenity key. Below you'll find some that fall into these categories, although there are others. To help activate and heal your relationship with this key, you might strike up a relationship with any or all of these deities. You might also wear jewelry depicting one of them, or create an altar to (or simply display an image of) one or more of them in the serenity area of your home.

BUDDHA

No other deity symbolizes stillness quite like the Buddha. Just as there is a complete, blissful stillness underlying everything in existence (even when we forget that it's there), it's said that we all have a Buddha residing in our heart. An image of a meditating Buddha (*not* a laughing Buddha—we'll talk about him in the prosperity key chapter) confers the energy of blissful stillness.

QUAN YIN

A feminine representation of Buddhalike energy, Quan Yin is known as a goddess of compassion. Her name means "she who hears prayers."

ATHENA

There is a part of us that is one with the Divine and that knows everything we need to know for every decision and situation. Athena, the Greek goddess of wisdom, helps align us with this powerful inner knowing that is our birthright.

GREEN TARA

A Tibetan goddess of empowerment and growth, Green Tara helps give us the incentive and willpower we need to make necessary life changes and stick to them.

WHITE TARA

Like Green Tara, White Tara is another aspect of the multi-faceted Tibetan goddess Tara. Her energy is very similar to Quan Yin's energy and is all about gentleness, sensitivity, purity, and compassion.

SARASVATI

Sarasvati is the Hindu goddess of wisdom, learning, and the arts. She can help us with learning new things, enhancing our skills, and mastering our chosen craft.

Serenity Key Animals

Like deities, each animal carries its own unique qualities and helpful energy. To activate the serenity key in your life, you can work with the animals below through meditation, prayer, altars, or imagery in your home (especially in your serenity area), on your altar, or on your person (as in jewelry or tattoos).

BEE

Hard, diligent work is an important aspect of self-mastery and self-cultivation, and when we work with the imagery and energy of bees, it infuses us with a very motivated sense of "go-go-go." This can be especially helpful if you want to jumpstart an exercise program or strengthen your motivation and initiative, or if you've recently increased your workload and want to hit a manageable stride.

OWL

The owl is traditionally associated with the goddess Athena (see page 40) and shares her alignment with wisdom, intuition, and that part of us that is one with the all-knowing Divine.

TURTLE OR TORTOISE

The turtle is traditionally believed to be the vessel through which the wisdom of the I Ching was presented to humans. The ancient Native American belief that the earth rests on the back of a giant turtle brings to mind the very grounded, still, earthy energies associated with the serenity key. And we all know that the most reliable and lasting way to learn new things is systematically, over time—as in "slow and steady wins the race."

Serenity Key Colors

To activate or enhance the serenity key in your life, you might work with any or all of the following colors, perhaps in one or more of the following ways:

- Wear one or more of them.

- Obtain a candle in one of the colors. Hold it in both hands and mentally charge it with a specific intention related to the serenity key (exercise, study, self-care, etc.) Then place it in the serenity area of your home, and light it.

- Decorate with two or more of the colors in the serenity area of your home.

  Spring, Sage, or Honeydew Green: Colors of springtime, life, and growth.

  Light, Robin's-Egg, or Cobalt Blue: Colors of peace, joy, and spirituality.

  Black: A color of depth, integrity, and introspection.

  White or Cream: Colors of the conscious mind, words, ideas, and precision.

  Brown, Beige, or Tan: Colors of grounding, nourishment, and connection to the earth.

Serenity Key Herbs

PEPPERMINT

Because of its cool freshness, and because it's simultaneously exhilarating and soothing, any kind of mint shares the energy of the serenity key and can help activate it powerfully in your life. Peppermint is especially energizing.

Try:

- Diffusing peppermint essential oil to receive its energizing and soothing aromatherapeutic benefits

- Drinking peppermint tea

- Placing a few fresh or dried
  peppermint leaves in a hot bath

SAGE

With a fresh, invigorating, centering aroma and a name that's a synonym for "wise one," this herb is a natural match with the serenity key. Try diffusing the essential oil of sage, misting a room with water into which you've placed 10–20 drops of essential oil of sage, or smudging a room with the smoke from a bundle of dried white or desert sage to infuse your home (and life) with blissful stillness and serenity.

ROSEMARY

Rosemary can wake up your mind and help you focus when you need to. That's why diffusing the essential oil or rubbing a bit of the fresh plant between your fingers and inhaling the scent can fortify you when you need to get a term paper done or for long nights of study before an important test. You might even bring a sprig of rosemary to class or waft an open bottle of the essential oil under your nose before the test itself. Rosemary can also help you anytime your mind needs a boost of clarity and acuity.

Serenity Key Crystals

To receive the serenity key–enhancing benefits of any of the crystals below, wear it, carry it, or place it in the serenity area of your home. You may also empower it with any of the serenity key affirmations from earlier in the chapter.

RUTILATED QUARTZ

Rutilated quartz can help clarify and energize your mind, fortify your self-improvement efforts, and enhance your confidence and self-esteem.

FLUORITE

Fluorite brings a minty freshness to the mind and can lend an exhilarating excitement to the early stages of a positive life change. It also helps instill a sense of calm serenity by subtly yet powerfully organizing our thoughts and consequently inspiring us to organize our lives.

AMETHYST

This beautiful violet-colored quartz has a highly spiritual and soothing energy that can increase your self-love, relieve anxiety, enhance and encourage meditation, and help you get a deep and restful night's sleep.

Serenity Key Master Ritual

If, after reading through this entire book once, you determine that the serenity key is the key that could use the most help in your life right now, performing the following ritual will help activate and calibrate this key for you in an ideal way. Or perform this ritual anytime when you discover that your serenity key is in need of some major help.

Because the art of bliss is a holistic science, not only will your serenity key benefit from this ritual, but every other life key will benefit as well.

INGREDIENTS

A white quartz or rutilated quartz point

Essential oil of peppermint

The night before the ritual, cleanse the quartz by bathing it in white sage smoke or holding it under cold running water for one minute.

On the morning of a new moon, wake up just before sunrise. Assemble the ingredients, and go outside where you will be able to see the sunrise. Sit comfortably, facing east. Take some deep breaths, relax your body, and get into as calm a state as possible. As soon as the sunlight peeks above the horizon, anoint your wrists, heart, and temples with a tiny bit of peppermint oil. (If you have sensitive skin, simply waft the bottle under your nose.) Then, while holding the crystal in your right hand, relax again and gently observe the continuing sunrise. When the sun has fully cleared the horizon, say:

> As this is the dawn of a new day for the planet,
> This is the dawn of a new day for me.
> Just as the sunlight is blindingly bright,
> The love I have for myself is immense,
> And henceforth I will treat myself as such.
> I will engage in immaculate self-care,
> I will follow my bliss,
> And I will in all ways honor the still awareness
>   that is underlying all that I think and perceive.

I now call on _____ *(insert the name of a serenity*
  key deity or animal of your choice) to align me
  with the energy of the serenity key,
And I now choose to embody the
  wisdom of this being.
I give thanks to the new day,
I give thanks to the new moon,
I give thanks to _____ *(serenity*
  key deity or animal),
And I give thanks to the harmony and
  balance that is the truth of my being.
Thank you, thank you, thank you.
Blessed be.
And so it is.

Until the next new moon, keep the crystal with you and anoint yourself with (or inhale) the peppermint oil every morning upon arising. When the moon cycle is complete, place the crystal in the serenity area of your home. Leave it there for as long as you feel as necessary (feel free to move it when you've sufficiently absorbed the benefits of the ritual).

2 | Life Path

You are alone in a tiny life raft way out in the middle of the ocean. Even though miles and miles of open water surround you in every direction, you find that you feel perfectly relaxed and not fearful in any way. As you gaze at the surface of the water, you notice that it ripples but is relatively still. You look beyond the surface and wonder how far down it goes and what lies in its very deepest depths. Your curiosity gets so strong, in fact, that you can't stop yourself from making the leap.

Although the water is extremely cold, you find the temperature to be comforting and somehow perfect. You also discover that you can easily breathe underwater. You swim down and down. Along the way, you notice and commune with sea creatures of all sizes—even sharks—without any fear. Soon, as you continue to descend, the water becomes dark, but because this is the ocean of your own emotions and soul, you are still able to see, although you don't have words for all you experience. You go deeper and deeper until you arrive at the farthest depths. Here you find your truest self and your most authentic joy.

**This is the alchemical essence
of life key #2: life path.**

If the energies associated with this life key are flowing harmoniously, the following statements will be true for you (and the more ideal the flow, the more true they will be):

- My regular activities are natural outpourings of my most authentic self.

- When I make important life decisions, I always consult and honor my inner wellspring of joy.

- My relationship with myself is characterized by integrity and honesty.

- I value my emotions and give myself space to feel my feelings.

- I remember my dreams and honor the lessons they teach me about myself.

- I value going beyond words and experiencing things directly, without having to name, analyze, or categorize every feeling and experience.

- I feel nourished by my activities, hobbies, and endeavors.

- I feel nourished by sharing my gifts with others.

- I can see how others are nourished
  when I share my gifts with them.

- I know what I truly love to do, and I
  can clearly see how expressing that love
  and following my passion can benefit
  the planet for generations to come.

- I embrace the mystery of life.

- I feel that I am in the flow.

Qualities Associated with the Life Path Key

Many people associate the term *life path* with one's job or career title. While choosing a career that is ideal for you is often a natural side effect of being in alignment with this life key, the outer appearance of a job or a job title is not the point. Most of us will have a whole bunch of jobs throughout our lifetime, and all the while we may be fulfilling the same life path, not only through our occupation as the world sees it but through charitable endeavors that we may do as volunteer work, artistic endeavors that we may do "on the side," and our everyday interactions with other humans, animals, and the planet.

In other words, when you're in touch with your depths (the life path key), all the waves—the things you do—originate from the same source and move in the same direction. You heal and bless the world simply by being yourself, and all your actions are pure, natural expressions of your authenticity.

The following descriptions are designed to help you to determine how well the life path key is already flowing in your life and also to begin creating subtle shifts that will prepare you to more fully activate it.

ENTERING THE MYSTERY

Who am I? Where did I come from? What am I doing here? What will happen to me after I die? While these timeless, universal human questions are relentlessly unanswerable in the conventional sense, when your life path key is activated and flowing, you wouldn't have it any other way.

If you look deeply, you can see that struggling against the mystery of existence might be seen as the primary source of human suffering and strife, while surrendering to it and embracing it might be seen as the primary source of human inspiration and joy.

CONSULTING THE WELLSPRING OF JOY

We often think of joy as being characterized by lightness, laughter, and happiness. However, when it comes to the life path key, we must remember that joy is also deep, poignant, and filled with every sort of emotion there is. It is evocative of the words of the magician-poet William Blake:

> Joy and woe are woven fine,
> A clothing for the soul divine.
> Under every grief and pine
> Runs a joy with silken twine.

When our hearts are truly open, every emotion—every smile, every tear, every victory, and every heartbreak—is characterized by joy. Joy is an aliveness, a depth, and a courage to be fully present in our lives—to feel our feelings and to let our emotions run deep.

It is this level of joy—the joy that encompasses the full spectrum of human emotion—that we get in touch with and draw upon when we are in alignment with this life key. Only then can we make decisions that nourish us, nourish other beings and the planet, and allow us to flow along our most ideal life path.

Decision-Making Exercise: WHICH WAY DOES THE WELLSPRING FLOW?

Although there are teachers and authority figures who try to tell us otherwise, when it comes to decisions, there is no "one way." No one has strengths and gifts exactly like yours, and no one can know which direction is right for you at any given time except you—but only when you consult your inner wellspring of joy.

Whether you're deciding where (or if) to go to college, which city or country to live in, what to make for dinner, or which shoes you want to wear with that outfit, your inner wellspring will point the way.

To begin, relax, take some deep breaths, and come fully into the present moment. Then consider your options—the things you are deciding between. Select one and imagine that you have chosen that option. From a feeling place (not a thinking place), notice how much water flows up from your wellspring of joy when you feel the feelings that go along with having chosen that option. How right does it feel? How "in the flow" does it feel? When this feels complete, repeat with each option.

If you're willing to override what we call logic and rational thought and follow the wellspring, you'll get into a lovely flow, and your decisions will lead you in exactly the direction your heart of hearts most wants to go. Speaking of which...

BEING IN THE FLOW

Just as a clear mountain stream flows effortlessly and constantly toward its source, our life path (when the life path key is activated) seems to have its own innate wisdom and moves continuously forward with an inner, divine momentum. This isn't to say that everything is easy all the time, but rather that the challenges we encounter are all a part of the flow—all a part of our soul's desire to learn and grow during this lifetime.

When we stop fighting against the flow that is our life path, even our struggles feel more meaningful and satisfying because we are nourished by our divine nature and internal wellspring of joy. The things we do on a regular basis are things that feel natural and essential, and they lead us organically along the path that our heart and soul most want to take.

AUTHENTICITY

When we interact with the world in an authentic way, we have nothing to fear. Our confidence is organic, because we have nothing to hide. And we make clear and definite decisions that propel us toward our hearts' desires because we are deeply rooted in the truth of who we are.

Checklist: AUTHENTICITY

Most of the time…

> …do you know what you want?
>
> …do you *do* what you want?
>
> …do you say no to things that
> don't feel right to you?
>
> …do you say yes to your heart's truest desires?
>
> …do you tell others what you think
> in a loving but firm way?
>
> …do you embody your truest ideals?
>
> …do you stand up for yourself?
>
> …do you believe in yourself?
>
> …do you believe that you have what
> it takes to live your dreams?
>
> …do you feel comfortable saying "I don't know"?
>
> …do you admit your strengths
> to yourself and others?
>
> …do you admit your weaknesses
> to yourself and others?
>
> …do you know that you are
> aligned with the Divine?
>
> …do you allow the Divine to flow
> through you in all that you do?
>
> …do you choose to identify with your
> true, divine self rather than your ego?

...do you choose to identify with your true,
divine self rather than the self you imagine
others *think* you should strive to be?

LEARNING FROM DREAMS

Like the life path key, dreams are aligned with the ocean
and with our dark, watery, mysterious, nonlinear depths.
Whether we consciously remember our dreams or not, they
help us sort out details, deal with fears, solve problems, and
make decisions. But when our life path key is activated and
flowing, we often remember our dreams and allow ourselves
to consciously receive messages from them that can actively
help us in our lives and more deeply align us with our most
ideal life path.

If you need help remembering your dreams, keeping a
dream journal or tape recorder next to your bed can help.
Later, when you consider the dream, see if you can intuitively
decode any important messages contained therein. Here are
some tips that can help with this process:

- What first comes to mind if you think "I
  wonder what this dream is about?" The
  author and dream expert Denise Linn says
  that a good way to override our linear
  thinking minds and access our intuition
  is to ask, "If I knew, what would it be?"

- When you consider the feelings and
  situations in the dream, what parallels can
  you see in your present life circumstances?

- Were there any motifs in the dream (things that occurred more than once, perhaps in a number of different guises)?

- Do you have the sense that you were dreaming of a past life? If so, how might the situation in the past life relate to your present circumstances?

- Do you have the sense that you were engaging in astral travel (i.e., do you have the sense that your etheric body left your physical body to roam the subtle component of the physical realm)? If so, where did you go, and what did you see? Did you feel empowered? Frightened? Curious? Joyful? How might your activities and feelings relate to your current state of mind and spiritual path?

GOING BEYOND WORDS

The part of our consciousness that is aligned with the life path key reaches much, much deeper than the part of our consciousness that labels and explains things with words. To illustrate, imagine that you're sitting on a beautiful beach. The sunlight sparkles on the water, the cool salt air caresses your face, and the waves roll eternally in and then out again. What is it within you that most authentically enjoys this moment? Is it the fact that you know the name of the beach? Is it the idea that you can later describe the color of the sand to your family over dinner? Is it the anticipation of bragging about your ocean visit to your friends or posting about it on a social media site? Of course not! It's something that goes far, far beyond words or explanation. In fact, it's something that is not diminished by words, though it can be temporarily obscured by them, as would be the case if you spent your entire beach visit thinking about what words you would use to describe the visit to your family. There would still be a deep, eternal part of you that would enjoy the visit in an authentic way, but your conscious mind would be all but completely obscured by your word-obsessed thoughts.

You might say that we live in a word-obsessed culture or that our species is at a word-obsessed stage in our evolution. The truth is, words are simply symbols: things that represent other things. But there is a lot of mistaking words for what they are meant to represent going around. The problem with this is that words are linear and exclusive, so when we mistake them for what they're meant to symbolize, it traps us in a linear and limited way of perceiving and interacting with the world. In fact, the world as we know it is unlimited, and contemporary theoretical physicists now attest that it is also nonlinear.

To use an example, many people are currently mistaking spiritual texts such as the Bible and the Koran for being literally true and holy in and of themselves. In other words, they are mistaking the words for what the words were originally meant to describe (since that's ultimately all words are good for), and as such are fostering things like exclusivity, prejudice, violence, and a persistent belief that the end times are imminent.

The Buddha prepared for this tendency of humans when he reminded his students that his teachings were pointing at the truth the same way a finger points at the moon. In the same way the finger was not the moon, the teachings were not the truth; they were simply pointing at the truth.

How does this all relate to the life path key? When the life path key is activated, we are free to feel and perceive on a level that is free of the tyranny of words. We still use words, but we don't feel bound or limited by them, and as such we are free to recognize and enjoy the full spectrum of our existence.

This helps us to know ourselves in a more intimate way and to be in touch with the intuition that leads us along our life's most joyful and satisfying path.

EMOTIONAL CONNECTION

Like the ocean, our tears are made up of saltwater. In order to know our hearts, follow our paths, and embrace our dreams, we must allow our emotions—even the painful ones—to flow. And, like the mysterious and unknowable ocean depths, sometimes the reasons for our emotions will be shrouded in mystery. We will feel like crying for no discernible reason, or a sudden, inexplicable flush of joy will arise upon hearing the name of a city or a country or considering a new possibility. This is our personal flow and the life path key giving us clues or simply reminding us that we are alive.

HONORING YOUR PASSIONS

Perhaps at the present moment you feel your time is taken up by a million things you don't really want to do but feel you have to do or should do. Perhaps this has been the case for so long, you're not even sure what you would do if you had all the time in the world.

Whether or not this describes you, it's important to set aside at least a little bit of time and energy almost every day for honoring your passions and doing the things that you love—even if it's only ten minutes. If you continue this practice over time and combine it with some of the alchemical practices outlined here, you will turn the tide for yourself, and, over time, you will begin to manifest more and more time and resources to devote to the things that you love.

Quiz: PASSION DISCOVERY

Not sure where your passions lie? Answer the following questions:

> If I had all the time and resources in the world,
>   what would I spend my time doing?
>
> If money were not an issue, what
>   career would I choose?
>
> What games did I like to play as a child?
>
> What fascinated me as a child?
>
> Who did I admire as a child?
>
> When I was a child, what did my
>   dream life look like?

What games did I like to play as an adolescent?

What fascinated me as an adolescent?

Who did I admire as an adolescent?

When I was an adolescent, what did
my dream life look like?

Now that I'm an adult, what
games do I like to play?

What fascinates me?

Who do I admire?

What does my dream life look like?

Now look over your answers and see if you can uncover any clues to your passion. Then, if you don't already, choose to honor them, and devote time to them now!

SPENDING TIME NEAR WATER AND
DRINKING LOTS OF WATER

Simply spending time near a body of water helps align us with the life path key. If you live near a body of water, even better. If you don't, be sure that you have water features (fountains, ponds, or pools) in and around your home. Even a little desk fountain can help. (See page 65 for placement ideas.)

Also be sure to drink at least half your body weight in ounces of pure water each day to keep your emotions, passions, and life path key flowing.

Life Path Key-Related Situations

Life situations and intentions that are related to the life path key include:

- Making important life decisions
- Making decisions based on internal factors rather than external factors
- Trusting and honoring your sense of inner knowing
- Making career-related decisions based on your inner wellspring of joy
- Getting in touch with your authenticity
- Staying in alignment with your authenticity
- Feeling your feelings
- Honoring your true self
- Following your bliss

Life Path Key Affirmations

I joyfully embrace the mystery of life.

I know just what to do because my inner wellspring of joy points the way.

I surrender to the natural flow of my life.

I happily allow myself to be who I am and do what I do.

I remember and learn from my dreams.

I experience life directly.

I allow my emotions to flow.

I allow myself to know what makes my heart sing.

I lovingly devote time and energy to the things
that bring me joy.

The Alchemy of Life Path

The degree to which we're aligned with our life path key constantly and eternally flows forth tangibly in the physical world, powerfully defining the way we experience our passions, our authenticity, our emotions, and our joy. Earlier in this chapter you became aware of this truth, which gave you the consciousness you need in order to alchemically align with this key and experience its benefits to an even deeper and more potent degree. When you're ready to swim even more deeply into your watery depths, the information in this chapter will guide your way.

Remember that there's no need to do every single idea presented here. If your intention is strong, just one or two will have a positive effect. But if you feel drawn to do more, go for it!

Life Path Key Symbols

THE NUMBER ONE

In the ocean, an unlimited number of waves arise and then disperse. For a fleeting moment they may appear to have a separate identity, but in the eternal sense they are nothing other than the ocean itself.

63

Similarly, we arise like waves or mist, but when we go beyond the surface appearance of our existence and go into the darkest depths of who we are, we discover that our current identity and life experience is simply a fleeting receptacle for the Divine, for the One.

The more we surrender to our true nature—the more we allow the Divine to flow through us—the more joyful and authentic we become. Like a stream flowing toward the sea, our path almost seems to choose itself, and we nourish everything we touch along the way.

The number one, whole and complete in and of itself, reminds us of our true, divine identity and aligns us with our divine power and our most ideal life path.

Here are some ideas for activating the life path key with the number one:

- Sit comfortably, with your spine straight, and meditate. Close your eyes and focus on your third eye (the area between and just above your eyebrows). As you inhale, think the word *all*. As you exhale, think the word *one*.

- Write the number 1 on an index card or small piece of paper and attach it to the back of a framed picture of the ocean. Then hang the picture in the life path area of your home. While standing near the picture, hold your hands in prayer pose (hands flat, palms touching at your heart). Close your eyes;

take three long, deep breaths; and then say: "I am one with the One." Then repeat the phrase ten more times, focusing on your thumbs, index fingers, middle fingers, ring fingers, and pinkies successively (two times) to keep count. Finally, feel and imagine that you are already aligned with the life path key in exactly the ways you desire. Hold this feeling for about thirty seconds to a minute.

THE OCEAN AND WATER

As we've already discussed, the ocean's deepest depths, the entirety of the ocean, and water in general are the classic symbols depicting the energy of this life key.

Here are some ideas for activating the life path key with them:

- Spend time near a moving body of water or take a trip to the ocean.

- Hang one or more paintings or pictures of the ocean in the life path area of your home.

- Hang one or more paintings or pictures of abundant waterfalls in the life path area of your home.

- Place a water feature, such as a fountain or ocean globe (like a snow globe, only ocean-themed), in the life path area of your home.

- Place an outdoor fountain in your front yard.

- Drink at least half your body weight
  in ounces of water per day.

- Take a long sea salt bath.

THE MOON

While the sun represents extroversion, activity, and the external world, the moon represents introspection, silence, and the world within. She's also aligned with the ocean's tides, the ocean's depth, and the ocean's cool, watery, mysterious energy. Naturally, this means that she is also aligned with the life path key.

Here are some ideas for activating the life path key with her:

- Sit outdoors in silent communion
  with the moon.

- Be aware of the phases of the moon. Celebrate
  new beginnings and plant new seeds at the
  new moon, feel your power and desired
  conditions growing during the waxing moon,
  celebrate the fullness of your power on the
  full moon, and consciously release and let go
  of what is unwanted as the moon wanes.

- Place 3–5 drops of Moon Milk (a
  planetary essence that can be found at
  www.keepingtime.net) under your tongue
  2–3 times per day or place 10 drops of
  Moon Milk in a warm bath and soak.

- Place moon imagery in the life
  path area of your home.

- Get a moon tattoo.

GLASS AND MIRRORS

Glass and mirrors have a watery feeling to them and are aligned with the water element in feng shui.

Here are some ideas for activating the life path key with them:

- Choose glass accents for the life
  path area of your home.

- Decorate with mirrors in the life
  path area of your home.

- Place glass marbles in decorative glass bottles
  or jars and place in the life path area of your
  home. Close your eyes and conjure up the
  ocean by visualizing/imagining/feeling it.
  Place your hands on the bottle or jar and
  mentally direct the energy of the ocean into it.

BLACK OR DARK GREY RIVER ROCKS

The smoothness, shape, and color of river rocks, along with the watery energy they embody, align them with the water element and the life path key.

Here are some ideas for activating the life path key with them:

- Decorate with river rocks in the
  life path area of your home.

- If your front door enters into the life path
  area of your home, make or purchase
  a doormat made with river rocks.

Life Path Key Deities

Divinities that are associated with authenticity, depth, water, silence, and solitude share the qualities and energy of the life path key. Below you'll find some that fall into these categories, although there are many others. To help activate and heal your relationship with this key, you might strike up a relationship with any or all of these deities. You might also wear jewelry depicting one of them or create an altar to (or simply display an image of) one or more of them in the life path area of your home.

LLYR/LIR

Llyr/Lir—the Welsh and Irish god of the sea, respectively—is the courageous chieftain of the divine fairy race called the Tuatha de Danann. Llyr/Lir embodies the deep, ancient, seemingly all-powerful energy of the ocean itself.

LUNA AND SELENE

Ancient forerunners to the Roman and Greek moon goddesses Diana and Artemis, Luna and Selene are more singly aligned with the moon and consequently have a more concentrated lunar energy.

NEPTUNE AND POSEIDON

Neptune and Poseidon—Roman and Greek, respectively—may be thought of as two different names for the same deity: the white-bearded, trident-carrying, stern yet magical king of the ocean deep.

SEDNA

Sedna is the Inuit goddess of the ocean: the old woman who dwells in the ocean's depths, the queen (and creatrix) of sea creatures, and the beloved mother of the sea. As is appropriate for an ocean-aligned deity, she is both beloved and feared.

SIGE

Sige is the Gnostic goddess of silence, stillness, introspection, and the place beyond words.

YEMAYA AND OLOKUN

In addition to being totally aligned with the upper parts of the ocean (and, according to some accounts, the entire ocean as well), Yemaya is the Yoruban incarnation of the Great Goddess and Divine Mother. Often appearing as an exquisitely beautiful woman with the tail of a fish (like a mermaid), she soothes, heals, cleanses, and showers us, her children, with the divine blessings associated with being in alignment with the life path key.

Sometimes considered another aspect, or polarity, of Yemaya and sometimes considered a separate deity, Olokun is the Yoruban god/dess (sometimes portrayed as male, sometimes as female) of unfathomable wisdom and the deepest parts of the ocean. As such, Olokun is a very potent embodiment of the energies associated with the life path key.

Life Path Key Animals and Magical Beings

Like deities, each animal or magical being carries its own unique qualities and helpful energy. To activate the life path key in your life, you can work with the animals and magical beings below (as well as other sea creatures) through meditation, prayer, altars, or imagery in your home (especially the life path area), on your altar, or on your person (as in jewelry or tattoos).

WHALES

The wise ancients of the deep, whales embody authenticity and oneness with the Divine.

FISH

As representations of equanimity, blessings, and water energy, fish can help us go beyond words to find and tap the abundant fountain of joy within.

SEALS

Seals represent dreams, intuition, and the subconscious. They can help us trust our intuitive guidance and align with the truth of who we are.

MER PEOPLE

Potent representations of shedding our obsession with the surface of things and gliding gracefully beneath the waves, mermaids and mermen inspire us to surrender our linear and language-based thought and fearlessly plumb our darkest depths.

Life Path Key Colors

To activate or enhance the life path key in your life, you might work with any or all of the following colors, perhaps in one or more of the following ways:

- Wear one or more of them.

- Obtain a glass or metal receptacle (with an airtight lid) in one of the colors. Fill it with water, and close the lid. Hold it in both hands and mentally charge it with a specific intention related to the life path key (insight into your most ideal career path, feeling your feelings, etc.). Then place it in the life path area of your home. Refresh it by charging it with your intention weekly until you feel you've manifested your intention, then pour it into a moving body of water.

- Decorate with two or more of the following colors in the life path area of your home:

   Black: The color classically aligned with the water element in feng shui and Taoist alchemy, black embodies authenticity, depth, downward movement, and flow.

   Navy, Cobalt, or Royal Blue: Also aligned with the water element, deep blues have a lighter, more joyful, and more buoyant feeling than black.

White or Cream: Although white and
cream don't symbolize the water element,
they are supportive of the water element
and allow it to gather and remain in
the way that a cup holds water. In other
words, when things that represent the
water element (symbols, colors, imagery,
etc.) are present, white or cream can help
them express their potency and power.

Charcoal Grey: As a color made up of black
(the water element) and a little bit of white
(a color that supports water), charcoal grey is
very evocative of water, the water element,
and the characteristics of the life path key.

Life Path Key Herbs

YLANG YLANG

Energetically speaking, the floral scent ylang ylang is
highly aligned with the water element and our own personal
watery depths. Inhaling it relaxes the mind and soothes the
defenses, allowing us to connect with our emotions, joy, and
inner knowing.

Try:

- Diffusing the essential oil in
  your home or workspace

- Misting your space with rose water into which
  you've added 10–20 drops of ylang ylang

- Adding a few drops to your bathwater

- Mixing the essential oil in a carrier oil like jojoba and anointing your heart and belly

WHITE ROSE

Sacred to the goddess Yemaya (see page 69), white roses share the purifying, healing energy of the sea.

Try:

- Bringing a single white rose to the ocean or another moving body of water. Call on Yemaya to help clear you of anything holding back from embracing your joy and fully activating your life path key. Lightly brush your forehead, throat, heart, and belly with the blossom, and then throw the flower into the water. Thank Yemaya for her help.

- Adding white rose petals to your bathwater.

KELP

Even if you live far from the ocean, adding kelp, dulse, or other types of edible seaweed to your food can help infuse you with its energy and that of the life path key.

Life Path Key Crystals

To receive the life path key–enhancing benefits of any of the crystals listed here, wear it, carry it, or place it in the life path area of your home. You may also empower it with any of the life path key affirmations from pages 62–63.

AQUAMARINE

Even though she's solid as a rock (and, in fact, *is* a rock), aquamarine's energy makes her as watery as they come. She's like saltwater sea foam and limpid, sunlight-infused tide pools. If you determine that, above all, your life path key could most benefit from a dose of clarity, purity, inner simplification, and a reconnection with your wellspring of joy, aquamarine might be just the crystal for you.

MOONSTONE

As you might expect, moonstone is aligned with the moon. This means her cool, receptive, introspective, and nourishing energy helps us tap into our intuition and emotions. Moonstone is a great help for those times when we feel overly rigid, out of touch with our feelings and sensitivity, or excessively focused on the external world. While at first it might seem that she throws us into greater discord or confusion, she ultimately brings balance by helping us break through and reconnect with our multidimensional consciousness and the unfathomable mystery of life.

BLACK TOURMALINE

When we feel like we're "all over the place" or have trouble focusing because we aren't really clear on what we want or who we really are, tourmaline can help. He not only aligns us with our watery depths and the life path key, but he provides a stable, grounding influence that assists us with crystallizing our vision, discovering our most ideal direction, and taking concrete steps toward our goals.

Life Path Key Master Ritual

If, after reading through this entire book once, you determine that the life path key is the key that could use the most help in your life right now, performing the following ritual will activate and calibrate this key for you in an ideal way. Or perform this ritual anytime you discover that your life path key is in need of some major help.

Because the art of bliss is a holistic science, not only will your life path key benefit from this ritual, but every other life key will benefit as well.

INGREDIENTS

> A part of the ocean that's safe for swimming
>
> OR a cold bath into which you have
> dissolved 2 cups of sea salt and placed an
> aquamarine crystal in a candlelit bathroom

If you're using the ocean:

Don your bathing suit (or skip it if it's a nude beach) and visit the ocean. Stand comfortably at the shore with your spine straight, and gaze out at the waves. Relax, take some deep breaths, and come into harmony with the ocean and the present moment. Say:

> **Great Goddess Yemaya, Great God**
> **Olokun, I call on you.**
> **Spirits and creatures of water and the**
> **ocean, I call on you.** *(Feel free to revise these*
> *names to suit your tradition and preference.)*

I now choose to align myself
　　with my watery depths.
I now choose to feel my feelings
　　and learn from my dreams.
I now choose to connect with my authenticity
　　and live from the truth of my being.
I now choose to nourish and bless the
　　world by flowing with the current
　　that my soul most wants to take.
I dwell in the place beyond words.
I go inward and find my unlimited
　　wellspring of joy.
I surrender to the mystery.
Great Ocean, I surrender.
Flow through me.

Now approach the ocean (run or walk as you see fit) and completely immerse yourself in the water. Say:

Thank you, thank you, thank you.
Blessed be.
And so it is.

You may then get out and dry off or remain in the water for as long as you wish.

If you're using a bathtub:

Once you've lit the candle, drawn the bath, and added the ingredients (as listed above), remove your clothes and stand next to the tub. Hold your hands in prayer pose at your heart, take some deep breaths, and come into the present moment. When you feel ready, visualize the ocean. Hear the sound of the waves, smell the salt water, and envision how it would look and feel to swim into its depths. Say:

Ocean, I call on you.

Hold your palms over the water and mentally send the energy of the ocean into the water through the palms of your hands. Say:

> **Water is water is water.**
> **I now recognize the interconnectedness**
>   **of this water and the water contained**
>   **in all the oceans of the world.**
> **I now see this water as the ocean and**
>   **I now see the ocean as this water,**
>   **for, in truth, they are one.**

Now intone the chant from the ocean ritual.

Immerse yourself completely in the water and say:

> **Thank you, thank you, thank you.**
> **Blessed be.**
> **And so it is.**

You may then remain in the water for as long as you wish, or get out and dry off.

3 | Synchronicity

You can sense that winter is on the way as a faint breeze sends a breath of chill across your skin. You look up into a vibrantly blue sky lit up with liquid-like golden-white sunlight and accented with glowing white clouds. And now you feel your spirit—the invisible essence of your being—leaving your body and ascending up, up, up, into this beautiful sky. You find yourself going above the clouds, out of the atmosphere, and into the realm sometimes known as heaven. From this viewpoint you can see every aspect of your earthly life with much greater perspective. You feel divine beings surrounding your etheric self even as you realize that they are observing and supporting your earthly life and helping orchestrate even the tiniest of details, always for your truest good and always only to the extent that your earthly self chooses to allow them to. You marvel as you observe that this help is available to you always, and you realize that this is, in fact, something that you have always known.

**This is the alchemical essence of
life key #3: synchronicity.**

If the energies associated with this life key are flowing harmoniously, the following statements will be true for you (and the more ideal the flow, the truer they will be):

- I am constantly amazed by how everything just seems to work out.

- I usually feel that I'm in the perfect place at the perfect time, doing the perfect thing.

- There are a lot of helpful people in my life.

- People seem to like helping me, and I am happy to receive their help.

- My life is filled with miracles and happy "coincidences."

- I love traveling, and I always seem to have the best luck with every aspect of my trips.

- I always find the best parking spaces.

- Without trying too hard, I usually arrive at the perfect time: not too early and not too late.

- I like the people I work for and with.

- I almost always have safe and reliable transportation to the places I want to go.

- I'm comfortable with technology and, when necessary, I generally have good luck fixing my gadgets/devices or having them fixed.

- My communication devices (phone, computer) are almost always in good working order.

- When connections would come in handy, I always seem to "know someone who knows someone."

- I enjoy helping others, and I do so on a regular basis for my own personal satisfaction.

- I don't feel like I have to "go it alone," and I remember to ask for divine help on a regular basis.

- I feel comfortable asking for divine help for even the smallest things.

- I trust that I will receive the perfect divine help at the perfect time, and I always do.

- I regularly notice signs and nudges from the universe, which I trust and happily follow.

Qualities Associated with the Synchronicity Key

The following descriptions are designed to help you determine how well the synchronicity key is already flowing in your life, and also begin creating subtle shifts that will prepare you to more fully activate it. As you read, be sure not to judge or berate yourself if these qualities don't perfectly match your current life experience. Instead, relax, perform any or all of the suggested exercises (as you feel moved), and allow the descriptions to infuse your awareness with the qualities they represent.

BEING IN THE RIGHT PLACE AT THE RIGHT TIME

Sometimes we can get caught up in the illusion of the hustle and bustle of it all and feel that we should be somewhere else, doing something completely different. Or perhaps we feel that we should be a bit further along on the road or in a different job than the one we're in or living in a different city or wearing a different outfit or dating a different partner or being more spiritually tuned-in or even being someone else entirely, perhaps a model or a movie star or a Nobel Prize winner.

The truth, of course, is that there is only one moment, and there has only ever been one moment: now. When we forget about that single moment—the now—and put all our attention on something outside of the now (that which is not), we are forfeiting the immense and singular joy of accepting and being present with what is.

In fact, the only way not to be in the right place at the right time is to think that you are not—to think that something should be different in order for you to be happy (you should be somewhere else, be doing something else, be somebody else entirely, etc.).

When we fully enter the present moment and accept it as it is now, we immediately realize that, in actuality, we are in the perfect place at the perfect time, doing the perfect thing. Once we realize that everything is perfectly unfolding right now in this very moment, no matter what appearance this moment may or may not take, little by little and more and more, we begin to discover that miracles are everywhere and that perfect opportunities are constantly appearing as a matter of course.

EVERYTHING "JUST WORKING OUT"

When things don't look the way we expected them to look or thought they should look (say, if it rains on the first day of a camping trip), before we even begin to decide what actions (if any) we want to take in the external realm, we do one of two things on the internal plane: we say an inner yes to the course of events or we say an inner no to them. When we say an inner yes, we are allowing the space for things to end up working out in an ideal and ultimately pleasing way. This doesn't mean that we don't take action on the physical plane if we feel moved (postpone the trip, stay in the tent and tell ghost stories, etc.); it just means that we begin by accepting that the flow of things might not always look the way we thought it would, and that this doesn't mean that it's necessarily worse than it otherwise would have been.

When we say the inner yes, we step out of the universe's way and allow divine orchestration to flow through us, guide our actions and the situation, and align everything in such a way so that it "all just seems to work out"—or at least so that we can accept, roll with, and find the blessings contained within whatever may unfold.

HARMONIOUS TRAVEL

When the synchronicity key is activated and flowing, traveling is fun, uplifting, and characterized by breeziness and ease. While everything might not end up looking exactly like we thought it would, we say an inner yes to adventure and allow the moment to be what it is and take us where it will.

GOOD TRANSPORTATION

If you feel comfortable with your transportation options— if they're generally safe, reliable, and get you where you need to go in good spirits and in perfect timing—it's a pretty good indication that your synchronicity key is going strong.

TECHNOLOGICAL EASE

Gadgets and machines, especially those that have to do with communication and connecting with others, also have to do with the synchronicity key. A harmonious synchronicity key means we're comfortable with our gadgets and we have good luck with fixing them or getting them fixed when necessary.

ASKING FOR HELP

Asking for help from beings in both the seen and the unseen realms is an imperative prerequisite to successful living. While it may sometimes seem that we are each just a single being against the world, nothing could be further from the truth. We are all one with each other and one with the Divine. The more we remember this, the happier and more successful we will be. Being reluctant to ask for help perpetuates the illusion of separation and the feeling that we are just one "little me," and asking for help reminds us that we are part of everything and, as such, that we are all-powerful. This opens the door to our power to truly effect positive change in our lives and in the world.

RECEIVING HELP

We must also be willing to receive help, whether it's help we've asked for or help that is freely offered to us. This doesn't mean, of course, that we have to accept help every single time it's offered, because sometimes we might genuinely prefer taking care of things on our own. But the more effortlessly and naturally we can say, "Yes, sure, I'd love help with this, thank you!" for even the little things in our life, the more we activate and enhance our synchronicity key, and the easier and more harmonious everything seems to become.

While in theory receiving help should be the easiest thing in the world, it can seem difficult sometimes because of the ego-generated illusion that there is value in refusing help and because of our society's misguided praise of "going it alone." In fact, even when we've asked, we can sometimes push help away when we hold the strong unconscious belief that we're the only power at work in our own life.

For example, if our family situation is characterized by fighting and discord, we might inwardly say, "Universe (or angels, or God/dess), please help! Please heal these conflicts and bring peace to every member of our family." Then, instead of releasing the problem and allowing the part of us that is one with divine wisdom take over, we might continue to act out of our ego and attempt to micromanage the seeming difficulties, which would, of course, only perpetuate the disagreements. Even if we stop all actions on the physical plane, if we continue to hold on to the outcome from an ego perspective (by saying an inner no to the appearance of things or thinking things like "But it wasn't supposed to happen this way!"), this is still an energetic message to the universe that roughly translates to "I know I asked for help, but actually it's okay—I've got this one."

But when we allow help in all forms by continuously releasing the ego's grip on things and by saying an inner yes to what is, everything begins to work better. Abundance flows, opportunities abound, and we realize that the moment is continually blossoming in a perfect (if sometimes unexpected or temporarily challenging) way.

Practice: ALLOWING HELP

One way to begin to get the hang of allowing help is to release the ego's grip by taking a deep breath and envisioning your entire body as a fist slowly unclenching and relaxing, releasing all seeming problems and worries to the Divine. The Divine then immediately swoops them up and transmutes them into the perfect unfolding of the moment. You might do this after requesting divine assistance, and then repeat it anytime you feel yourself holding on.

RECEIVING NUDGES AND GUIDANCE

One very important way we receive help from the universe (or God, Goddess, All That Is, etc.) is in the form of nudges and guidance. For example, three separate people on three separate occasions may casually mention New York City in conversation, and you suddenly get the hint that it's time to finally take that trip to New York. Or you might inwardly just know something, like "It's time to look on Craigslist for a new apartment *right now*"—and follow your hunch to discover exactly the right place for exactly the right price. We all receive this guidance all the time, but when we're alert to it and let it guide us to our most ideal life conditions, we're totally in alignment with the synchronicity key and all the blessings that go along with it.

PROVIDING HELP

Just as we must exhale in order to inhale, providing help to others with an open heart creates space in our life for blessings to flow right back to us in abundance. This doesn't mean sacrificing, being martyrs, or forcing ourselves to help in ways we don't feel comfortable with. It means asking, "How can I personally—with my talents, abilities, and possessions—most be of service right now in a way that brings me joy?" This may include an entire spectrum of things, like holding the door for someone, offering a smile to a stranger, helping a friend move, donating time or money to charities you feel good about, expressing art in a way that can heal and support others, and ultimately seeing your entire life as a means to bring blessings to the world.

HELPFUL PEOPLE

As a matter of course, do you expect people—people you already know and people you've just met—to be helpful and friendly? And, generally speaking, do they meet those expectations? If you answered yes to both questions, it sounds like your synchronicity key is in pretty good shape. (But if you answered no to either or both, never fear! You'll find plenty of information in the remainder of this chapter to help you turn this around.)

GOOD CONNECTIONS

The old maxim "it's not what you know, it's who you know" is incorrect. We all know that, in fact, it's what you know *and* who you know (not to mention where you are, what day of the week it is, how prepared you are, and a whole collection of other contributing factors). And being connected to the right people at the right time under the right circumstances all have to do with that divine perspective and flow that so perfectly characterizes the synchronicity key.

Synchronicity Key-Related Situations

Life situations and intentions that are related to the synchronicity key include:

- Trips and journeys

- Driving and parking

- Attracting customers and clients

- Finding and obtaining a job

- Finding and obtaining employees or contractors

- Interviews and meetings

- Any situation that can benefit from positive relationships with others

- Interacting with your coworkers and colleagues

- Interacting with your landlord/landlady, contractors, delivery drivers, and other people in positions to make your life easier

- Working with technology and communication devices
- Communicating and connecting with others
- Engaging in teamwork of any kind

Synchronicity Key Affirmations

I am always in the perfect place at the perfect time doing the perfect thing.

Everything is perfectly unfolding.

I am in divine flow.

I ask for and receive divine help with everything.

I am totally open and receptive to receiving divine help.

I am awake and alert to my divine guidance, which I immediately trust and immediately follow.

I am always surrounded by the friendliest and most helpful people.

I love and support everyone, and everyone loves and supports me.

It is safe for me to receive help from others and the Divine.

I now happily experience perfect, divine orchestration in every area of my life.

Everything is easy, breezy, and harmonious.

I enjoy my trip and arrive at my destination safely, happily, and in perfect timing.

I say yes to the moment.

The Alchemy of Synchronicity

Carl Jung, father of psychology, occult scholar, and the coiner of the term *synchronicity*, wrote: "In all chaos there is a cosmos, in all disorder a seeming order."

The philosopher Seneca wrote: "Luck is preparation plus opportunity."

The synchronicity key and the information in this chapter is about discovering and flowing with the order within the seeming disorder, creating the space for opportunity, being prepared when opportunity knocks, and creating our own "luck."

Synchronicity Key Symbols

THE NUMBER SIX

In order to sense the connection between the number six and the heavenly realm (and the synchronicity key), all you need to do is think about snow. Each sparkly white six-sided flake is a heavenly gift and love note to earth: a drop of the Infinite temporarily appearing in the form of a tiny ice flower. And the number six demonstrates its alliance with helpful friends and the sweetness of harmonious teamwork when it appears as the repetitive and interlocking hexagrams of a honeycomb. Both incarnations of the number, along with the mathematical qualities of the number itself (e.g., the number's connection to circles—see below), demonstrate heavenly order and divine orchestration.

Here are some ideas for activating the synchronicity key with the number six:

- Decorate with one or more hexagrams or snowflake patterns in the synchronicity area of your home.

- Create an attractive grouping of six crystals (see page 105 for crystals associated with the synchronicity key) and place it in the synchronicity area of your home. (Be sure to cleanse them initially and then at least once a month by running them under cold water and then bathing them in white sage smoke.)

- Place six small crystal beads (see page 105 for ideas) on a chain or a cord. Cleanse the crystals, and then hold them in both hands and mentally empower them with synchronicity energy by repeating one of the affirmations from earlier in the chapter six times. Wear around your neck or wrist. Repeat the empowerment procedure after cleansing.

THE SKY AND HEAVENLY REALM

As we've already discussed, the sky and heavenly realm are the classic symbols that depict the energy of this life key.

Here are some ideas for activating the synchronicity key with them:

- Recline outdoors and relax your mind as you gaze at the sky and marvel at its vastness.
- Display one or more pictures or paintings of the sky in the synchronicity area of your home.
- Display one or more pictures or paintings of stars, planets, or galaxies in the synchronicity area of your home.
- Connect with the vastness of the sky and request divine assistance before journeys or anytime you need help with synchronicity-related issues.

ANGELS AND OTHER HELPFUL BEINGS

Angels, as quintessential divine helpers and residents of the heavenly realm, resonate powerfully with the synchronicity key. So do other types of angel-like helpers, such as spirit guides, favorite deities, and even beings in the earthly realm that act like angels by swooping in to offer divinely designed help at just the right time.

Here are some ideas for activating the synchronicity key with them:

- Remember to call on your divine helpers to help you with everything! You might call on them immediately upon awakening and throughout the day by saying something as simple as "Angels, please help!" or "Goddess, I could really use your help with this one" or "Divine beings of light, please help me with everything today." Then remember to allow the help by releasing ego attachments to the outcome, being open to any guidance you may receive, and taking guided action as you feel moved.

- Place angelic imagery in the synchronicity area of your home.

- Place imagery related to divine beings or spirit guides in the synchronicity area of your home.

- In the synchronicity area of your home, decorate with imagery depicting two or more people or animals who appear to be supporting each other or working together in helpful harmony.

CIRCLES, SPHERES, AND OVALS

The heavens appear as a glorious and highly orchestrated dance of spheres and ellipses, so it should come as no surprise that according to a number of ancient magical practices—including feng shui and sacred geometry—circles, spheres, and ovals represent the realm of heaven.

Here are some ideas for activating the synchronicity key with them:

- When attractive and appropriate, decorate with circles, spheres, or ovals in the synchronicity area of your home (in prints, pictures, sculpture, furniture, etc).

- Choose a round or spherical pendant made of metal or one of the crystals described in this chapter. Cleanse it with sage smoke and empower it by holding it in both hands and repeating one of the synchronicity key affirmations six times while visualizing/ imagining/feeling it filled and pulsating with very bright white light, then wear it.

METAL

If all metal suddenly vanished from the earth, we would no longer be able to travel by bike, car, plane, or train. We also would no longer be able to use mechanical watches, telephones, televisions, or computers. (And the list goes on and on!) Obviously, our access to metal—and its potent synchronicity key energy—has allowed us to cultivate an uncommon mastery of mobility, precision, communication, and speed.

Here are some ideas for activating the synchronicity key with metal:

- When attractive and appropriate, choose metal accents and objects to display in the synchronicity area of your home.

- Empower a piece of metal jewelry
  by holding it in both hands and
  repeating one of the synchronicity key
  affirmations six times, then wear it.

GADGETS AND TECHNOLOGY

One need only reflect on the life of Nikola Tesla to realize that the inventions and discoveries that underlie the technology that shapes our culture are derived from direct downloads of divine inspiration. Not only that, but this same technology weaves connections between us, improves communication, and infuses our society with the ability to harmonize our efforts at a faster rate and on a more effective level than ever before. (To illustrate, consider the successful Facebook-fueled revolutions in Egypt and across the Middle East.)

Here are some ideas for activating the synchronicity key with them:

- Regularly, perhaps on Monday morning or as a
  part of your daily meditation, bless your phone
  and computer with the energy of harmonious
  communication and divine orchestration. To
  do this, visualize the gadget being filled with
  very bright white light, then say something
  like this: "Angels, please bless this _____
  (computer, phone, etc.) and empower it
  with the energy of harmonious, helpful, and
  loving communication. I now dedicate this
  computer/phone/etc. to divine flow and the
  perfect unfolding of everyone's truest good."

VEHICLES

While we may take things like cars and planes for granted at this stage in history, the truth is that they are nothing short of miraculous. Like mechanical magic carpets with wheels, they whisk us from here to there in ways even our relatively recent ancestors could not have believed were remotely possible. Not only that, but they're made of metal, composed of machinery, and rolling on circles: veritable powerhouses of synchronicity key energy! (Bikes and skateboards fit into this category too.)

Here are some ideas for activating the synchronicity key with them:

- Daily, bless your vehicle of choice with synchronicity key energy. You might do this by visualizing a sphere of very bright white light completely filling and surrounding your vehicle. Graciously request that six angels stand watch over it at all times, keeping everyone in and around it safe. (Then be sure to thank them and to trust that they are indeed doing so.)

MAPS AND GLOBES

Maps and globes are aligned with the synchronicity key because they allow us to see the big picture. They show us where we are and where we want to go, and they remind us that we can, in fact, get from here to there.

Here are some ideas for activating the synchronicity key with them:

- Display decorative maps or globes in the synchronicity area of your home.

- Transform your globe into a synchronicity charm and be the king or queen of your world. When the moon is between new and full, either when the moon is in the sign of Sagittarius or on a Wednesday (or both), bathe your globe, along with six white quartz points, in white sage smoke. In the synchronicity area of your home, position the crystal points in a symmetrical circle around the globe, with each point pointing inward. Place your hands on either side of the globe so that they are hovering about an inch or two away from touching it, and say: "By divine right, I am queen (king) of my world. With endless and infinite divine orchestration, I reign. I am always in the perfect place at the perfect time, doing the perfect thing, and all good things come to me now." (Be sure to cleanse the quartz points with smoke or cold running water at least once a month.)

SACRED SMOKE

With fragrant smoke that makes the invisible visible and moves upward into the realm of heaven, incense and smudge sticks help merge our intentions with divine energy and orchestration.

Here are some ideas for activating the synchronicity key with it:

- Light a bundle, or smudge stick, of dried white sage and shake to extinguish the flame so that it's smoking rather than burning. While carrying a dish to catch burning embers, move in a counterclockwise direction throughout every room and area of your home. This will harmonize and purify the space in your home and align it more directly with the realm of heaven and the synchronicity key.

- Smudge the front door and all the thresholds of your home while repeating, inwardly or aloud: "My way is clear, my road is open, and my transitions are smooth."

- Light incense on your altar or elsewhere. As you do so, inwardly declare that it's a fragrant offering to your angels, one or more helpful beings in the unseen realm, or the entire realm of heaven.

Synchronicity Key Deities

Although divine help in general is associated with the synchronicity key, divinities that are associated with travel, the heavenly realm, and swift, divine assistance are especially in alignment with this key. Below, you'll find some that fall into these categories. To help activate and heal your relationship with this key, you might strike up a relationship with any or all of them. You might also wear jewelry depicting one of them or create an altar to (or simply display an image of) one or more of them in the synchronicity area of your home.

ARCHANGEL MICHAEL

Archangel Michael is the captain of the angelic realm. Swift, Powerful, Protective, and Helpful (all capitalized!) are his middle names. And talk about orchestration! Simply calling on Archangel Michael when you get up in the morning and anytime throughout the day can infuse you and every situation in which you find yourself with harmony, flow, empowerment, and success.

GANESH

How could a divine being with the moniker "The Remover of Obstacles" not be powerfully associated with the synchronicity key? Strong yet benign, efficient yet calm, this dearly beloved elephant-headed deity of the Hindu pantheon goes before us to make our way swift, harmonious, and successful by potently decimating any obstacles that may have previously littered our path. That's why he's traditionally invoked at the beginning of projects and journeys.

ISIS

Isis, the Egyptian mother goddess, keeper of magic and mysteries, and mistress of sacred sexuality, wields a power that is immense and all-encompassing. Make no mistake: if Isis is your ally, your way will be smoothed and your endeavors will receive a divine infusion of success. She is not, however, one to call on lightly or one who just shows up for everyone who casually calls on her. She prefers a certain level of devotion, so aligning with her energy requires a bit of time and effort. If you feel drawn to working with her, spend time studying her mysteries, offering her devotions (creating an altar to her, burning incense to her, etc.), and meeting her in meditation. She can be especially helpful for women who are trying to balance busy schedules to have plenty of time and energy for both home and work and for anyone looking to merge their femininity with their strength.

ST. CHRISTOPHER

St. Christopher was said to carry people across a river as part of his dedication to his spirituality. It's also said that when he carried a child across who claimed to be Christ, the child instructed him to place his staff in the earth, which then turned into a living, fruit-bearing palm tree. Now the patron saint of travelers, he's invoked for safe and pleasant journeys, and statues of him are buried near entrances and bridges to smooth transitions and protect thresholds.

HERMES

The Greek god of travel, magic, divination, and changes of fortune, Hermes powerfully correlates with the synchronicity key. Piles of stones were erected to him at crossroads and near entrances to bless travelers and facilitate auspicious transitions. Like Isis, he's not one to call on in a pinch but is more one to align yourself with in a deep and abiding way through ongoing devotion and contemplation. The benefits of doing so include an increased ability to sense divine guidance, be in the right place at the right time, follow the flow of your luck, and consciously affect your reality.

Synchronicity Key Animals

Like deities, each animal carries its own unique qualities and helpful energy. To activate the synchronicity key in your life, you can work with the animals below through meditation, prayer, altars, or imagery in your home, on your altar, or on your person (as in jewelry or tattoos).

BIRDS OF FLIGHT

As earthly emissaries from the heavenly realm, it might be said that flying birds are the angels of the animal kingdom. In fact, in countless cultures throughout history, people have looked to birds for divine guidance and spiritual messages. While different types of birds are said to represent different types of messages, if a bird flies noticeably into your world and it feels like a divine message of some sort, you might simply ask yourself (as the author Denise Linn recommends): "If I knew what you were trying to tell me, what would it be?" Still, it can also be helpful to be aware of the established symbolism of specific types of birds. While all flying birds are aligned with synchronicity key energy, the following few are especially so:

> **Eagle:** You are blessed and filled with divine energy itself. You and your efforts are aligned with the Divine.

Hawk: You're on the right path. Wisdom, foresight, and an awareness of the big picture are available to you now if you are open to them.

Falcon: Listen to the divine messages that are all around you. Are you listening? The Divine is attempting to get your attention.

Raven: You are spiraling into an awareness that includes more than the earthly realm. Quiet your mind and allow this stretching of your consciousness.

Crow: Go beyond time, the fear of death, and the appearance of limitation. This is where all power resides and is available to you.

Synchronicity Key Colors

To activate or enhance the synchronicity key in your life, you might work with any or all of the following colors, perhaps in one or more of the following ways:

- Wear one or more of them.

- Obtain a candle in one of the colors. Hold it in both hands and mentally charge it with a specific intention related to the synchronicity key (divine alignment, harmonious travel, receiving the right help at the right time, etc.). Then place it in the synchronicity area of your home, and light it.

- Decorate with two or more of the colors in the synchronicity area of your home.

  Whites and Creams: The heavenly realm, precision, protection

  All Shades of Grey: Divine flow, harmonious thinking

  Metallic Colors: Communication, swift action, divine orchestration

Synchronicity Key Herbs

ANGELICA

Angelica's angelic, sunshiny energy is bright, protective, and helpful.

Try:

- Placing a white or off-white sachet or drawstring bag of angelica in the synchronicity area of your home to protect the household, clear the energy, smooth and harmonize transitions, and diffuse peaceful vibrations.

- Diffusing essential oil of angelica for the same purpose.

GARLIC

The nutritional, culinary, and magical powerhouse of the herbal kingdom, garlic's protective and harmonizing powers are legendary. Empower a head of garlic in sunlight for 1–5 minutes. Then try:

- Holding it in both hands and repeating:
  "I am in divine flow; my journey is
  safe, and my way is clear" six times.
  Then place it in your suitcase.

- Holding it in both hands and
  repeating any of the synchronicity key
  affirmations six times. Then place it in
  the synchronicity area of your home.

- Holding it in both hands and repeating any of
  the synchronicity key affirmations six times.
  Then cut one clove from the head of garlic
  into tiny pieces and swallow them like pills.
  Repeat each day until the cloves are gone.

NETTLES

Among herbs, few (if any) are "sharper" than nettles. Magically speaking, this translates into precision, exactitude, and
harmonious orchestration. Try mentally empowering your
nettles with the energy of the synchronicity key by holding
the bag or jar in both hands and visualizing the herb being
filled with bright white light. Then try:

- Traveling with a sachet of dried
  nettles in your purse or suitcase.

- Sprinkling dried nettles on top of things like
  documents, brochures, or business cards related
  to situations you'd like to infuse with divine
  flow and synchronicity key energy. Then place
  in the synchronicity area of your home.

- Attaching a tiny sachet of nettles to your rearview mirror to facilitate smooth travel and mechanical excellence.

Synchronicity Key Crystals

To receive the synchronicity key–enhancing benefits of any of the crystals below, wear it, carry it, or place it in the synchronicity area of your home. You may also empower it with any of the synchronicity key affirmations that appear earlier in this chapter.

WHITE QUARTZ

With pure, concentrated divine energy and positive vibrations, white quartz is the synchronicity key in mineral form. Simply carrying a white quartz crystal point increases your spiritual energy field and improves mental power and focus. When consciously employed for your chosen purpose, it can also help with any intention related to the synchronicity key.

HEMATITE

Another mineral that has to do with precision and focus, hematite also vibrates in alignment with the synchronicity key in that it helps with being in the right place at the right time, divine intervention, harmonious flow, and success in all endeavors.

ANGELITE

Angelite is beautiful heavenly blue crystal that shares its energy with that of the angelic realm. When we have one on our person or in the room, we more easily sense our connection with angels and we more easily allow ourselves to receive angelic protection and support.

PYRITE

Simply holding pyrite immediately aligns you with both grounding earth energy and the swift assistance associated with the heavenly realm. As such, pyrite helps all your earthly endeavors to be infused with heavenly orchestration.

Synchronicity Key Master Ritual

If, after reading through this entire book once, you determine that the synchronicity key is the key that could use the most help in your life right now, performing the following ritual will activate and calibrate this key for you in an ideal way. Or perform this ritual anytime you discover that your synchronicity key is in need of some major help.

Because the art of bliss is a holistic science, not only will your synchronicity key benefit from this ritual, but every other life key will benefit as well.

INGREDIENTS

> 6 frankincense incense sticks
>
> One half of an unpeeled orange
>
> A large dinner plate
>
> A bundle of dried white sage
>
> A jar with a lid that seals tightly
>
> A lighter or matches

After showering or bathing, dress in all-white, 100 percent clean clothes. With your ingredients in tow, climb up to a high point with a good view, with little or no fire danger, where you won't be disturbed: a cliff, a mountaintop, or a roof. (If this is not possible or practical, choose another spot—even if it's indoors—and simply take a moment to visualize climbing up to a high viewpoint and looking down.)

Assemble the ingredients in front of you. Relax (sitting or standing), close your eyes, and take some deep breaths. When you feel centered, open your eyes and place the orange, flat side down, in the center of the plate. Light one stick of incense as you say:

> I light this incense as an offering to the
> Divine and to the heavenly realm.

Now stick the end of the incense in the orange in such a way that the ashes will fall straight down or onto the plate. Repeat five more times with each stick of incense.

Now say:

> Divine realm, realm of heaven, you are
> here now, as you have always been,
> always waiting to rush to my assistance
> and orchestrate everything beautifully,
> down to the tiniest detail.
> I am here because I am now choosing to
> accept this help: to align with you and
> to lock into my most ideal flow.

I know that I am worthy of accepting this
help because, in truth, you and I are
one; because what is best for me is also
best for you; because what is best for
me is also best for all of existence.
I now pledge to listen to my intuition, to
follow my guidance, and to trust that
everything is perfectly unfolding.
Thank you for meeting me where I am
and helping me to establish this habit.
Thank you for harmonizing my life
and powerfully infusing it with
synchronicity and flow.

Now light the bundle of sage and shake off the flame so
that it's smoking (not burning), and bathe yourself from head
to toe in the smoke. As you do so, know that you are cleansing yourself of all blocks to receiving divine help and fully
aligning with the synchronicity key. When this is complete,
seal the sage in the jar to extinguish. Finally, say:

I am now aligned.
I am now in the flow.
Now doors open for me everywhere.
I happily walk through these doors,
and my life magically unfolds.
Thank you, thank you, thank you.
Blessed be.
And so it is.

4 | Creativity

With childlike joy, you splash around in a sparkling lake, which reflects the deep blue sky and the fluffy white clouds. You are in perfect harmony with the golden koi fish that swim beneath you, the swans that glide around you, the lily pads, the brightly colored flowers, and all the seemingly mythical plants and animals that animate this whimsical landscape. Like a child at play, you are completely lost in the fun and fullness of the moment.

**This is the alchemical essence of
life key # 4: creativity.**

If the energies associated with this life key are flowing harmoniously, the following statements will be true for you (and the more ideal the flow, the more true they will be):

- I feel comfortable expressing my thoughts, feelings, needs, and desires to others.

- I communicate clearly, peacefully, and effectively.

- I love speaking, writing, or singing.

- I love expressing myself through creative outlets such as painting, dancing, writing, music, etc.

- I approach everything I do with a spirit of playfulness and fun.

- I feel that life is a joyful adventure.

- I have my own unique style, and I take great joy in dressing and accessorizing in my own unique ways.

- I feel satisfied with my creative endeavors and my creative possibilities.

- I have a never-ending supply of ideas.

- I am spontaneous and love trying new things.

- I laugh deeply, organically, and often.

- I love discovering new ideas and new ways to look at things.

- I am awake to issues and traumas from my childhood that may be affecting my current life, and when they come up I proactively work to heal, unravel, and release them.

- I enjoy the journey of healing my inner child more and more deeply.

- I have a wonderful, natural, playful, mutually respectful relationship with my inner child.

- I am comfortable birthing, nurturing,
  or adopting new projects, people,
  and animal companions, and I do
  so in the ways I most desire.

- (If applicable) I have a wonderful, natural,
  playful, mutually respectful relationship
  with my children or animal companions.

Qualities Associated with the Creativity Key

The following descriptions are designed to help you determine how well the creativity key is already flowing in your life, and also to begin creating subtle shifts that will prepare you to more fully activate it. As you read, be sure not to judge or berate yourself if these qualities don't perfectly match your current life experience. Instead, relax, perform any or all of the suggested exercises (as you feel moved), and allow the descriptions to infuse your awareness with the qualities they represent.

HEALING AND HONORING THE INNER CHILD

Once we progress out of childhood, where does that child go? Does she (or he) just dissolve into the ether and disappear forever? Of course not; she stays with us and lives in our heart of hearts. Without her, we would never lose ourselves in fun or laugh until tears roll down our face or think of "out of the box" ways to do things. But often our inner child is still wounded from things that transpired long ago. Perhaps she is crying or confused or feels abandoned or unsafe.

But there is good news too: now that we are adults, when we consciously connect with our inner child, we can help heal her in all the ways she most needs to be healed. We can give her reassurance, protection, attention, unconditional love, uninterrupted playtime, or whatever else she has been craving for so many long years. In turn, this will begin to activate our creativity key and enhance our happiness, joy, relationships, and overall enjoyment of life.

Sometimes this can seem difficult, especially when we have a childhood we think we'd prefer to forget. But, for the sake of our bliss, it's imperative that we bring our unhealed childhood issues to the forefront of our consciousness so that we can heal them and allow our inner child to experience the lighthearted joy that is her birthright.

Practice: INNER CHILD INTERVIEW

If you're not sure what your inner child needs, ask him! Grab a notebook and a pen, then relax in a comfortable position, place your hands lightly over your heart area, close your eyes, and take some deep breaths. For a few moments, bring your awareness to your heart center (sternum area). Then envision yourself as a child somewhere between the ages of two and seven; whatever age feels right or naturally appears is best. Just as you would with a child in the physical realm, introduce yourself and begin to get acquainted in a way that feels right to you. Be aware that your inner child may appear relaxed and ready to talk right away or he/she may appear distressed and in need of some comforting and reassurance before he/she is ready to open up. Be open to whatever you discover, and take the time you need to connect. This step is very useful in and of itself.

Once your inner child is comfortable and ready to talk, ask him (or her) these questions, and then relax and listen to his answers. They may surprise you!

- How do you feel?
- Do you feel safe?
- Is there anything I can do to help you feel safer?
- Do you feel happy?
- Is there anything I can do to help you feel happier?
- What would you like to do more of?
- What would you like to do less of?
- What do you need that you didn't get from grownups before?
- How can I give that to you now?

Sometimes just listening and becoming aware is all that is needed in order to begin healing. Other times you may want to start regularly setting aside time to draw, paint, or play, or perhaps your inner child would like for you to take a trip to a museum or park, or for you to spend more time consciously connected to him, or for you to get her a special treat.

Of course, your inner child is still a child, so it's not appropriate for him/her to run the show. The trick is to balance the inner child's needs for playfulness and healing with your adult sense of order and responsibility. For example, she might tell you she wants to dance all day and eat candy for every meal, in which case you might respond, "Sometimes we'll need to do other things besides dance, but we can begin to set aside time to dance once a day. And it wouldn't be healthy to have candy for every meal, but we can definitely get a candy bar after dinner!"

Afterwards, be sure to jot down anything you'll want to remember later—information received in this way has a reputation for leaving the conscious mind rather rapidly, sort of like a dream.

(PS: If this exercise seems silly to you, that's all the more reason to do it!)

Practice: INNER CHILD EXCAVATION WORK

Many of us come into adulthood feeling beset by relatively serious childhood issues at every turn. To use myself as an example, my parents got a divorce when I was four. Later, I was molested by my (former) stepfather. Additionally, all throughout my childhood, a number of challenging adult figures played central roles and seemed to move in and out of my life rather rapidly.

As you can imagine, this led me to feel extremely untrusting of others, unsafe, and generally psychologically out of sorts in a number of ways. For many years, my inner child definitely didn't feel playful or free (at least not in a balanced way). Even to this day, I still find myself uncovering more and more old leftover paradigms and limiting beliefs that are ready to be released so that I can experience the present and future as something wonderful and entirely new.

But the cool thing is that now I feel invigorated by this process. I know that every time I discover this old leftover "stuff," I bring it into the light. As the shadows disappear, I realize that there's nothing to be afraid of. These old issues no longer have power over me. Then, after gaining clarity and doing the necessary inner work, I let go and experience a delicious feeling of freedom and bliss. In effect, this is alchemy in and of itself: by bringing courage and attention to these old, painful feelings, we can transmute them into a deeper experience of wisdom, presence, and joy than otherwise would have been possible.

Sometimes—when you feel your inner child asking to be heard, when you're craving emotional healing, or when you feel that you're ready for an emotional breakthrough—it can be helpful to go deep. You might think of this like clearing inner clutter, organizing your old memories and emotions, and creating a beautiful play space for your inner child's imagination and creativity to soar.

Here's one of the best ways I've found to do this: set a timer for half an hour or an hour. Call up the first memory that pops into your mind from childhood. It might be a seemingly good memory or it might be a seemingly bad memory. The important thing is that it holds an emotional charge and feels like it wants to be examined and heard. Then just write it out. What is the memory exactly? How did you feel? What colors, pictures, facial expressions, etc., do you associate with it? Don't be concerned with the quality of your writing or your writing style—just write for its own sake. You can use your computer or a notebook, whatever feels right.

If an emotion comes up during this process, good! Go through it. Don't attempt to go around it or stop before you get to it. Keep writing until the time is up. You can stay with the same memory or move on to another one, whatever feels right.

Be sure to drink lots of water during and after the writing period. You might want to repeat this daily for a while, or three times per week, until you feel you've gained the perspective and healing you've been craving. This might be a process that you stay with for months or even years, or one that you find yourself coming back to again and again.

(You'll find more guidance about healing old childhood issues in chapter 8.)

APPROACHING EVERYTHING WITH A
SENSE OF PLAYFULNESS AND FUN

You may be thinking, "Surely she's not suggesting that we should approach *everything* with a sense of playfulness and fun?" And you're right. I'm not suggesting that you should approach everything with a sense of playfulness and fun. But I am suggesting that you *could* approach everything with a sense of playfulness and fun.

And yes, I do mean everything.

I am not saying this lightly. I am very much aware of times that are generally not supposed to be thought of as playful. My family owns a funeral chapel, and my brother and I used to run around the chapel while my dad was embalming or making funeral arrangements. When grieving families were present, the secretaries shushed us harshly and dragged us out of sight.

Now, I don't mean to say that laughing and playing in the presence of grieving people is appropriate behavior (necessarily). What I do mean to say is that when we take a step back from the seeming Seriousness Of Everything, we can see that, in fact, all of existence is an exquisite, playful, swirling, sparkling, etheric finger painting that fades away into nothingness just as quickly as it appears.

From this perspective, one can feel one's grief fully at a funeral while still, on some level, experiencing the adventure and playfulness of simply being alive and experiencing life. After all, no matter what's going on, you've never experienced anything quite like this moment before, and you never will again.

Even so-called mundane tasks like doing the dishes or standing in line at the DMV can become magical, playful adventures when we get in touch with our inner child. As children, how many times did we take joy out of pretending we were grownups doing everyday things like mowing the lawn or vacuuming the floor? Well, now we *are* grownups! So how much more fun will it be for our inner child when we let her share our awareness? The daily grind can become transformed into a romp in the sandbox.

This idea of approaching everything with a sense of playfulness and fun also asks us to choose our activities wisely. If something doesn't feel fun to you, ask yourself why you do it, then examine the reason. If it's a functional reason, like "I wash the dishes so that I can have clean dishes when I need them," see if you can find a way to make washing the dishes more fun. A new, delicious-smelling dish soap, perhaps? A special song you always listen to as you wash? Or possibly you can just adopt a new, more playful perspective.

Some seemingly functional reasons, however, might not actually be functional upon further examination. For example, "I go to work so that I can pay the bills." There are many kinds of work you can find yourself doing. Why are you going to that one specifically? By looking more deeply, you might uncover a deeper "reason" such as, "I go to this particular work because I have no other choice." Is this really true? Perhaps tomorrow it's true to some degree, but, in truth, there are infinite possibilities about what kind of work you might find yourself doing. In this case, it might be that you learned a limiting belief about work from your parents or adopted some societal idea that was never really yours to begin with.

It is my belief that for every person there is at least one form of "work" that is actually the most delectable form of play. It's also my belief that when we engage in work that feels playful to us, we use our divine talents in the ways that most benefit the planet. And, no matter what, whenever we discover that our work is just plain hard, grueling work, there is always something we can do to increase the play factor, whether it's finding a new perspective about our current position, finding another gig that feels more playful, or begin-

ning to channel our efforts into manifesting a new, more satisfying career.

(For more help with getting in alignment with your most
ideal life path, see chapter 2.)

SPONTANEITY

When we lock ourselves into same-old, same-old expectations, our experience of life becomes hollow and wooden.
Our relationships suffer because we interact with our past
experiences and concepts of the person rather than the living,
breathing person standing in front of us. In all life areas, we
feel stuck in a rut, and experiencing everyday joy sounds like
an impossible dream.

When, on the other hand, our creativity key is activated
and flowing, we experience joy as a general rule because we
are aware that possibilities are endless and opportunities are
abundant. We are awake to the miracle of life. We know that
if we can imagine it, we can create it! We adventurously forge
new roads, create new conditions, and follow the path of our
joy. Even seemingly inconsequential situations and occur-
rences begin to feel pregnant with delightfully mysterious
potential.

IMAGINATION AND WHIMSY

Albert Einstein said, "Imagination is more important than
knowledge," and perhaps that's because without imagination,
knowledge would be stagnant: it wouldn't have any room
to expand. After all, how can you create something—or discover or formulate it—without the capacity to imagine? And,

perhaps more importantly, how can you enjoy life without allowing your imagination to play with the infinite possibilities posed by the mystery of existence?

When we were children, imagination was a way of life. Our imagination was never "just" our imagination—it was our world! Now that we're adults, to keep our intellectual thinking fresh and useful, and to enjoy our life to the fullest, it's important that we consciously nurture our imagination and allow it to soar.

Journal: IMAGINATION JUMPSTART

If you find yourself in a rut of overseriousness, or you don't know where to begin when it comes to nurturing your imagination, grab a notebook and write freely about your answers to the following questions.

As a child between the ages of two and five...

What were your favorite movies?

What were your favorite books?

What were your favorite toys?

What did you like to dress up as for Halloween?

What games did you like to play?

What did you like to pretend?

What did you draw pictures of?

As a child between the ages of six and ten...

What were your favorite movies?

What were your favorite books?

What were your favorite television shows?

What did you like to dress up as for Halloween?

What did you want to be when you grew up?

What did you do in your free time?

What did you draw pictures of?

Now see if you can get in touch with the joy associated with some of these memories, and think about ways that you can bring this joy into your adult life in some small ways. For example, as a child, I loved the book *The Secret Garden* and anything to do with castles, fairies, magic, and mythical creatures. As an adult, I celebrate these interests in many ways, including:

- Spending time with flowers and having silent conversations with them.

- Practicing natural magic, creating charms, and weaving spells.

- Going on vision quests (imagination-rich meditations) to the realm of the fey.

- Reading fantasy novels.

DEEP, ORGANIC LAUGHTER

When I was just out of high school, instead of going to a traditional college, I went to acting school. As an actress, I learned very quickly the difference between real laughter and forced laughter—not just from those on the stage but also from those in the audience. When you hear real laughter, it opens you up. Your muscles relax, and you feel happier. You might even start to giggle. Forced or nervous laughter, on the other hand, is a mirthless sound. It's like the difference between real flowers and plastic ones, and if you tune in, you can feel it in your gut.

Children, and especially babies, let laughter bubble up out of them like a crystal-clear mountain spring. Although they may not consciously be aware of it, this laughter opens up a door to the realm of the Divine. This provides healing not only for them but also for everyone in the general vicinity. In turn, this sends healing vibrations out into the unified field of energy and improves the frequency of the entire planet.

Indeed, in addition to being simply one of the best things on earth to experience (as if that weren't enough!), organic laughter has been clinically proven to provide physical healing in measurably potent ways.

When our creativity key is activated in an ideal way, we experience this sort of profound, magical laughter on a daily (or almost daily) basis.

Priming the Pump: LAUGHTER YOGA

As paradoxical as it may sound, consciously forcing laughter for a pre-set amount of time can begin to relax your diaphragm and open you up to the real thing. So if it's been too long a time since you've laughed down to your gut, you might like to try the following exercise.

When you're all by yourself, put on some fun, relaxing, and uplifting music. You might also like to light a candle or two or otherwise set the mood. Then sit or lie comfortably and close your eyes. Take some deep breaths and go through your entire body, relaxing completely. Pay special attention to your stomach and diaphragm area, and also your sternum and throat areas. When you feel very relaxed, set a timer for three minutes. Then place one hand lightly on your diaphragm and one hand lightly on your belly and begin to laugh rather loudly. As you do so, feel your diaphragm and belly going in and out, and consciously allow the vocalization of the laughter to originate in these areas of the body. Continue until the timer goes off.

You'll find that this process immediately improves your mood and makes you feel lighter and more buoyant. And it causes natural laughter to arise much more readily!

If necessary, repeat this process daily until your pump is primed and true laughter bubbles up often and of its own volition.

SPEAKING YOUR TRUTH WITH LOVE

The creativity key is about self-expression in all its many forms. This includes speaking your truth with love.

While we don't need to tell everyone in our life all our secrets and every little thing that crosses our minds, when our creativity key is activated and flowing, we speak up for ourselves, set healthy boundaries, and express our feelings and needs in ways that allow us to be heard and respected in the ways our soul craves.

The best secret I've found to learning to speak your truth with love is with a book. If speaking your truth with love is a special challenge for you, in addition to working with the exercises in this and the following chapter, I suggest reading the book *Nonviolent Communication* by Marshall B. Rosenberg. It's amazingly helpful for this purpose!

SATISFYING CREATIVE EXPRESSION

Everyone is a creative person! The idea that some people are creative and others are not is simply a myth. So whether you prefer to cook, sew, write, paint, draw, dance, act, direct, make music, or create in any other number of ways, it's important that you do so on a regular basis. For the purposes of the creativity key, it doesn't matter whether you channel your creativity into what you call your career or what you call your hobby: the important thing is that you channel it. (Although when we approach everything in the spirit of playfulness, even so-called mundane tasks begin to be charged with magic and creative energy.) Creative juices, like water and bliss, want to flow!

EXPRESSING YOUR UNIQUE STYLE

Trends and fashions are the results of waves of energy moving throughout the planet, affecting time periods and regions with a distinct flavor and essence. But these waves of energy affect everyone differently. While they may inspire some of us to wear flowy scarves and move to the countryside, others may be inspired to wear combat boots and move to the heart of the city. While I could write a whole book on this dynamic alone, the point is that regardless of what waves of energy are moving through at any particular time, we always have the opportunity to tune in to and celebrate our unique and ever-changing sense of style. And when our creativity key is activated and flowing, we do just that as a matter of course. We ride the wave of the shifting tide, allow our perspectives to stretch and alter, listen to the music that sounds good to us, and wear exactly what we feel like wearing, exactly when we feel like wearing it—whether we found it at the trendiest boutique or the mustiest thrift store in town.

Practice: HAVING FUN WITH FASHION

Divide a notebook page into three columns. At the head of the first column, write: *It might be fun to wear…* At the head of the second column, write: *If I were a little braver, I would wear…* And at the head of the third column, write: *I have always wanted to wear…* Now, without thinking about it too much and without stopping, finish each sentence, again and again, all the way down the page. Did you get any new ideas? Did you uncover any secret fashion dreams that might finally need to be brought out into the open? Maybe it's time for a trip to your favorite boutique or thrift store.

AN INFINITE WELLSPRING OF IDEAS

There is a limited aspect of our mind—what we might call our ego, or "little me"—and then there is an unlimited aspect of our mind, the part of us that is one with the Divine, with All That Is. And true creativity, while it in many ways flows through the appearance of the former, originates in the latter. So, because the Divine is infinite, when our creativity key is activated in an ideal way, our supply of ideas is infinite. It is like we're a faucet that is connected to a wellspring that never runs dry. If we want to create and express ourselves artistically, all we have to do is open the channel and be ready and willing to do the work (or, more accurately, *play*) that presents itself.

OPENNESS TO NEW IDEAS AND PERSPECTIVES

If we think we know it all or have finally got it all figured out, eventually our life will start to feel boring and stagnant. This is because the fresh, fluid, sparkling, playful, spontaneous energy of the creativity key has ceased to flow through our consciousness in a harmonious way. No matter how old we are, if we want to experience joy, we must still be open to learning, growing, listening deeply, and looking at things in new ways.

HARMONIOUS RELATIONSHIPS WITH
CHILDREN OR ANIMAL COMPANIONS

When our creativity key is activated and flowing, we have harmonious and conscious relationships with our children and animal companions. And if adoption or conception is a goal of ours, we are moving toward it or manifesting it in the most ideal ways possible.

Creativity Key-Related Situations

Life situations and intentions that are related to the creativity key include:

- Creating art
- Having ideas for creative projects
- Planting seeds for new projects and life conditions
- Finding creative solutions to "problems"
- Gaining new perspectives
- Spending time with children
- Spending time with animal companions
- Making the most of your "free time"
- Doing things just for the fun of it
- Seeing work as play
- Enjoying life
- Taking vacations
- Playing

- Laughing
- Lightening up
- Expressing yourself in harmonious and peaceful ways
- Child adoption
- Conception
- Animal adoption

Creativity Key Affirmations

Life is a joyful adventure.

I embrace the journey of life.

Life is fun.

I follow the path of fun.

Everything is an opportunity for joy.

I step into the flow of endless possibilities.

I allow myself to play.

I dance through life with lighthearted freedom.

I am free to be myself.

I express myself with joy.

I speak my truth with love.

I now give birth to new ideas and beautiful life conditions.

I am a sacred vessel of creation.

I am a channel of divine creativity.

I plant the seeds of joy.

The Alchemy of Creativity

As you've definitely figured out by now, if we want to activate any given key, we can begin to do so by consciously infusing our lives with the alchemical associations and properties of that key. And, no matter what key we are focusing on, one might say that our alchemical undertaking is a function of the creativity key. After all, the alchemy of bliss is a method of transforming the entire process of life into one giant art project: something with an endless supply of possibilities—something magical, playful, and fun.

Creativity Key Symbols

THE NUMBER SEVEN

The colors of the rainbow—along with the chakra system and the New Age "spiritual rays"—are generally recognized as appearing in seven distinct colors: red, orange, yellow, green, blue, indigo, and violet. There are seven days of the week, seven planetary energies (and associated metals) in classical alchemical teachings, and seven groups of crystal structures. Seven also appears in the moon cycles and is associated with the moon, which has been aligned with creativity and inspiration since ancient times. In short, seven is an alchemical superstar, representing the swirling, sparkling interplay of universal energies from which we can draw when consciously creating, whether we're creating art, children, or our personal reality.

Additionally, as six's successor, seven contains and defines divine energies just as we personally give life and definition to the divine energies that flow through us when we create art and share new ideas.

And, as numbers go, seven is unique and eccentric. It does not conform to patterns as easily as the other numbers, and in that way it mirrors our ability to stand on our own and express our personal style and flair.

Here are some ideas for activating the creativity key with the number seven:

- Empower seven crystals with one or more intentions related to the creativity key, and place them in the creativity area of your home. (Perhaps choose the variety from the list of crystals later in this chapter or, alternatively, choose one in each color of the rainbow. Or just choose a type that feels right to you for your intention.)

- Create or find whimsical artwork containing seven of some image that feels appropriate— seven hummingbirds, seven butterflies, seven frogs, seven flowers, etc.—and place it in the creativity area of your home.

- Create a creativity key activation charm with seven beads: white, cream, metallic, or one in each color of the rainbow. You might

make your charm in the form of a bracelet
or necklace, or hang it near your workspace
or in a window in your creativity area.
Remember to empower it with your intention.

SPARKLING WATER AND WATER IMAGERY

As we've already discussed, a sparkling lake setting is the classic symbol depicting the energy of this life key. Similarly, fountains, waterfalls, and other types of clean, radiant water (both actual and in image form) possess the energy of the creativity key.

Here are some ideas for activating the creativity key with water and water imagery:

- Place an attractive and beautiful-sounding
  desk fountain or larger indoor fountain
  in the creativity area of your home.

- Place images of lakes, waterfalls, or fountains
  in the creativity area of your home.

- Add a pond, waterfall, or fountain to your yard.

- Empower an aquamarine crystal or crystal
  pendant by holding it under or placing it
  in a clear, sparkling brook or waterfall for at
  least three minutes. Then keep it near you.

RAINBOWS AND RAINBOW COLORS

For most of us, rainbows (like dolphins, butterflies, and baby animals of all types) instantly inspire a pure, potent rush of childlike joy. They allow us to see the alchemy that underlies light, including all color and appearance of form. In other words, they allow us to glimpse the (usually) unseen artistic palette of the entire seen world.

Here are some ideas for activating the creativity key with them:

- Hang a faceted, prismatic crystal in a sunny window in the creativity area of your home.

- Decorate with rainbow colors in the creativity area of your home.

- Relax, close your eyes, and envision yourself completely cocooned in and filled with a sphere of bright red light. Repeat with orange, yellow, green, blue, indigo, and violet.

FAIRIES

Fairies and the creativity key are two peas in a pod. As the mystical beings that promote fun in all forms, urge us to enjoy life, have a special relationship with children and animals, and animate and embody the magic of nature, fairies couldn't be any more evocative of all that the creativity key represents.

Here are some ideas for activating the creativity key with them:

- Create a fairy altar in the creativity area of your home.

- Place fairy imagery in the creativity area of your home.

- Leave offerings for the fairies in nature or in your yard (they like shiny things, sweets, and bubbly drinks in small cups or walnut shells).

- Call fairies into your life and home, and ask them for help with your creativity key–related objectives.

WHIMSY

As you might imagine, whimsy—as in anything that gives your childlike imagination a boost—also shares the energy of the creativity key.

Here are some ideas for activating the creativity key with whimsy:

- Decorate the creativity area of your home with whimsical artwork.

- Read a book or watch a movie that excites your whimsical imagination (perhaps try *Alice in Wonderland*, *Where the Wild Things Are*, or *The Mists of Avalon*).

- Close your eyes, and, using your imagination as your vehicle, visit a mystical land. If you're looking for a creative breakthrough, an infusion of joy, or an answer to a seemingly unanswerable question or problem, you might consider asking one of the inhabitants of this land for advice.

CIRCLES, OVALS, ELLIPSES, AND EGG SHAPES

Circles, ovals, ellipses, and egg shapes possess the energy of seeds, birth, and regeneration. They represent contained thought and inward movement as they prepare to burst forth into new perspectives, projects, and creations. These shapes also are evocative of lakes, ponds, and small bodies of water, all of which share the energy of the creativity key.

Here are some ideas for activating the creativity key with them:

- In the creativity area of your home, choose round shapes for tables, pillows, mirrors, rugs, patterns, etc., when possible and appropriate.

- To help give birth to new perspectives and conditions or to bring in more joy, carry or wear an egg-shaped pendant.

CRYSTALS, ROCKS, AND METAL

In the I Ching, the oldest book and earliest known documentation of the alchemy of bliss, while the synchronicity key is associated with "greater metal," the creativity key is associated with "lesser metal" (as in the metal element of Chinese medicine and Taoist cosmology). Metal is the element of thought, precision, inward movement, and the realm heaven and the unseen. Physical representations of the metal element include gemstones, rocks, and metals of all types.

(This greater/lesser metal is mirrored in the way that angels are associated with the synchronicity key, while fairies are associated with the creativity key. In other words, "greater" and "lesser" are not value judgments but illustrations of the way the element manifests energetically.)

Here are some ideas for activating the creativity key with them:

- When decorating the creativity area of your home, choose crystal, metal, or rock materials when possible and appropriate.

- Place crystals in the creativity area of your home.

- Empower crystals or crystal jewelry with creativity key–related intentions and then carry or wear them.

Creativity Key Deities

Divinities that are associated with creativity, art, color, birth, harmonious communication, alchemy, and springtime share the qualities and energy of the creativity key. Below you'll find some that fall into these categories. To help activate and heal your relationship with this key, you might strike up a relationship with any or all of them. You might also wear jewelry depicting one of them or create an altar to (or simply display an image of) one or more of them in the creativity area of your home.

OSTARA

Ostara, the goddess from which Easter got its name, is the divine personification of birth, springtime, fertility, and new ideas.

MERLIN

It's hard to think of a deity more aligned with the creativity key than Merlin. After all, not only is he the archetypal magician, alchemist, and master energy worker, but he's also the playful trickster from the Arthurian legends. Using the spectrum of color, he works in the invisible realm to balance and fine-tune energies, and to get energies moving in the most ideal and joyful of ways.

BLUE OR MEDICINE BUDDHA (BHAISAJYAGURU)

Although Bhaisajyaguru is not traditionally associated with fun, joy, lightness, or creativity per se, he has repeatedly appeared to me as I write this chapter and seems to be insisting that he wants to be included in this section. His deep-blue color certainly evokes the joy and magic of the creativity key, and the fact that this color is often associated with lapis lazuli further validates the playful, childlike energy he seems to exude. He would like us to know that his healing work (what he is traditionally known for) is accomplished through a gentle and playful manipulation of the universal energies, which leads to a lightness of spirit, a highly calibrated energy, and, ultimately, vibrant physical health.

Creativity Key Animals

Like deities, each animal carries its own unique qualities and helpful energy. To activate the creativity key in your life, you can work with the animals below through meditation, prayer, altars, or imagery in your home, on your altar, or on your person (as in jewelry or tattoos).

HUMMINGBIRDS
Hummingbirds help us experience joy, lightness, freedom, and the sweetness of life.

BUTTERFLIES
In addition to lightness, magic, and whimsy, butterflies evoke transformation and remind us to be our own creations and to let our true selves soar above the same old–same old.

DRAGONFLIES
Dragonflies and fairies share the same energy, and, to my way of thinking, dragonflies actually *are* fairies (albeit one of the most commonly sighted varieties).

FROGS
Where there are joyful, sparkling lakes, there are usually frogs. They hop, glisten, sing, and generally embody the fertility and the clean, clear, sparkly wetness of the creativity key.

GOLDFISH AND KOI
Like frogs, koi and goldfish are like glistening, luxuriant jewels that delightfully populate the effervescent lake that is the creativity key, animating it with richness, life, movement, and possibility.

Creativity Key Colors

To activate or enhance the creativity key in your life, you might work with any or all of the following colors, perhaps in one or more of the following ways:

- Wear one or more of them.
- Obtain a candle in one of the colors. Hold it in both hands and mentally charge it with a specific intention related to the creativity key (communication, art, self-expression, etc.). Then place it in the creativity area of your home, and light it.
- Decorate with two or more of the colors in the creativity area of your home.

  White or Cream: Lightness, potential, mental power, and inward movement

  Silver or Metallic: Thoughts, imagination, precision, and the unseen world

  Bright, Light Blue, or Turquoise: Joy, self-expression, upward movement, and water

  Rainbow Colors: See page 131.

Creativity Key Herbs

YLANG YLANG

Ylang ylang's watery, joyful, sensualizing, highly vibrating, sky-blue scent connects us with our creativity, our spontaneity, and the realm of all possibility.

Try:

- Diffusing essential oil of ylang ylang in your home or near your workspace.

- Putting 3–6 drops essential oil of ylang ylang in your bathwater.

- Anointing your throat with essential oil of ylang ylang to help you express yourself creatively and to speak your truth with love.

MINT

Mints of all varieties are cool, fresh, and healing to the mind, body, and spirit, much like the sparkling, joyous bodies of water associated with this area. They also awaken our inspiration and motivation for creative self-expression.

Try:

- Adding fresh mint leaves to your bathwater.

- Diffusing essential oil of peppermint or spearmint in your home or near your workspace.

- Adding a little bit of peppermint oil to your body wash or lotion to invigorate you and infuse you with playfulness, spontaneity, and joy.

BERGAMOT

This unique herbal/citrus scent is simultaneously comforting and exhilarating, and it awakens and invigorates the creative mind.

Try:

- Diffusing essential oil of bergamot in your home or near your workspace.

- Drinking a cup of Earl Grey tea (black tea flavored with bergamot).

- Wafting an open bottle of essential oil of bergamot under your nose to awaken you to creative solutions, fresh perspectives, and new possibilities.

DESERT SAGE

The smoke of desert sage, or sagebrush, has a playful trickster energy. It opens the doors to new possibilities and conditions while inspiring the comfort and trust that allow the inner child to heal and thrive.

Try:

- Burning a bundle of dried desert sage (so that it's smoking, not burning) and moving around your home or workspace to create new possibilities, inspire spontaneity and play, and open yourself up to your divine creative flow.

Creativity Key Crystals

While all crystals and rocks can be thought of as related to the creativity key, the crystals described here are a sampling of some that resonate especially with the energy of this key.

To receive the creativity key–enhancing benefits of any of the crystals below, wear it, carry it, or place it in the creativity area of your home. You may also empower it with any of the creativity key affirmations that appear in this chapter.

LAPIS LAZULI

This true blue stone is like a crystallized version of a vibrant lake sparkling joyfully in the sunshine. It evokes feelings of playfulness and helps heal children and inner children.

RAINBOW QUARTZ

Any white or clear quartz with visible sparkly rainbows in it is a rainbow quartz, and rainbows, as we've seen, deeply embody and evoke the energy of the creativity key.

MOONSTONES AND OTHER SPECTROLITES (AKA LABRADORITE)

The soft, dreamy, rainbowy, whimsical nature of spectrolites helps us connect with our imagination, our inspiration, and our artistic flow.

AQUAMARINE

Aquamarine has the fresh, clean, fluid energy of a waterfall, bubbling brook, or sparkling lake, and it can help us heal our inner child, lighten up, and remember to play.

CHRYSOCOLLA

Self-love, self-expression, and comfort with speaking your truth are all enhanced with this gorgeous teal and turquoise stone.

AQUA AURA

A white quartz treated with gold at a very high temperature turns a vibrant, otherworldly aqua color and becomes what's known as an aqua aura. When it comes to creative expression, honest and direct communication, healing the inner child, awakening your playfulness, and gaining the confidence to go your own way, aqua aura is an amazing ally.

Creativity Key Master Ritual

If, after reading through this entire book once, you determine that the creativity key is the key that could use the most help in your life right now, performing the following ritual will activate and calibrate this key for you in an ideal way. Or perform this ritual anytime that you discover that your creativity key is in need of some major help.

Because the art of bliss is a holistic science, not only will your creativity key benefit from this ritual, but every other life key will benefit as well.

INGREDIENTS

An aqua aura crystal

Essential oil of ylang ylang (added to a carrier oil like jojoba if you have sensitive skin)

A cup of fresh mint leaves

2 soy candles

On the night before the first morning in a new moon cycle, light the candles and draw a bath. Add the mint leaves. Remove your clothes and, by candlelight, hold your hands over the water as you say:

> Merlin, I call on you.
> Fairies and realm of the fey, I call on you.
> Please infuse this water with your
>   magic and your rainbow light.
> May this water draw out and neutralize
>   any old poisons from the past so that my
>   inner child can be healed and free.
> May it refresh my spirit, liberate my
>   inspiration, clear my communication
>   channels, and fill me with joy.
> Thank you, thank you, thank you!

Now soak for at least forty minutes. Dispose of the mint leaves at the base of a tree or in a compost pile.

The next morning, awake before sunrise. After quickly jotting down any dreams you may remember (even if they're only images or don't make sense to you right now), take the ylang ylang and aqua aura outside with you and face east. (If the weather would make this too wet or uncomfortable, just stay inside and face east.) The minute the sun peeks above the horizon, anoint your brow, heart, and wrists with the oil. While holding the aqua aura to your heart with your right hand and covering your right hand with your left, sit or stand comfortably in silence as the sun continues to rise.

Then say:

> It is the dawn of a new day.
> My inner child is awakened.
> I clearly hear and follow my guidance about
>   how to pamper, heal, and protect my inner
>   child and to allow her (him) to skip (or
>   run or dance) joyfully through the world.
> I create as I feel guided, and I find
>   great joy in creative work.
> Everything I do is play, and I approach
>   everything with a spirit of fun.
> I speak my truth with love, and I communicate
>   in peaceful ways that are both gentle and firm.
> I draw from the magic of creation and weave
>   its beauty into the fabric of my world.
> I draw from the harmony of the spheres
>   and the alchemy of color, and I expertly
>   formulate the life of my dreams.

Keep the aqua aura with you for at least one moon cycle, and anoint your brow, heart, and wrists with the ylang ylang oil every morning for the same duration.

5 | Romance

It's a comfortably warm late summer afternoon. You and a beloved romantic partner are reclining on a soft blanket in an open meadow surrounded in the distance by green trees that create soft music as they sway. Wildflowers in yellows, oranges, deep pinks, and reds pepper the landscape among golden foxtails and wild oats. As birds sing melodically in the distance, you inhale the fresh, earthy fragrance in the air and feel relaxed down to your very soul. You know that the beauty that surrounds you reflects your own beauty, and vice versa. You feel held, cradled, and adored, not only by your partner but also by the Earth Goddess herself. Because you feel loved so dearly simply for being yourself, you know that if you wanted to, you could go anywhere, do anything, and face anyone; you feel that all doors are open to you and that everything is conspiring to assist you and bring you joy. Despite this knowledge, at this particular moment, you are certain that there is absolutely nothing that needs doing: that the best thing you could possibly do is relax and take it all in.

**This is the alchemical essence
of life key #5: romance.**

If the energies associated with this life key are flowing harmoniously, the following statements will be true for you (and the more ideal the flow, the truer they will be):

- I find it easy to relax and enjoy life's sensual pleasures.

- I appreciate the beauty in each moment.

- I see beauty in everyone I meet.

- I feel loved and adored by the people and animals in my life.

- I love and adore the people and animals in my life.

- I stop and smell the flowers (literally and figuratively).

- I know the value of well-spent leisure time.

- I know the value of spending time with my loved ones.

- I treat myself to things like massages and vacations.

- I enjoy receiving gifts and compliments.

- I enjoy surrounding myself with beauty.

- I enjoy engaging in beauty-enhancing activities.

- I feel pleased and comfortable with my current relationship or dating situation (regardless of what it is or isn't).

- I feel comfortable with my sexuality.

- When I look in the mirror, I feel pleased.

- On a normal day my face has a relaxed and receptive look to it.

- On a normal day my body is in a relaxed and receptive posture.

- On a normal day my breathing is relaxed.

- I feel grounded and serene.

- I enjoy discovering ways to enjoy life more.

- I love taking time to savor a delicious meal.

- I know that pleasure is valuable and healing.

Qualities Associated with the Romance Key

The following descriptions are designed to help you determine how well the romance key is already flowing in your life and also to begin creating subtle shifts that will prepare you to more fully activate it.

SENSUALITY

According to physicist James Lovelock's well-documented Gaia Theory, the entire planet, including all life on earth, is one unified, self-regulating organism. When we feel the truth of this down to the tips of our toes—that we are one with Mother Earth—our senses awaken. We feel at home in our bodies and free to enjoy the blissful sensory orchestra that we are a part of.

Not only does this activate our enjoyment of life, but it also enhances our attractiveness and magnetism.

Practice: SENSUALITY TUNE-IN

Take some deep breaths and relax. Now feel the sensual pleasure of simply being in your body: your gentle weight upon your chair, the feeling of your hair against your neck, the relaxing feeling of breath in your chest and belly, the delicious smell of your own perfume.

ENJOYMENT

Sometimes it seems as though our culture teaches that working hard and getting things done are the main purposes of life, and that enjoyment is just a diversion that has no real meaning or worth. When we examine this belief, we can see that it is obviously flawed. Can you imagine someone on her deathbed telling you that she wishes she just could have spent a little less time enjoying the moment and a little more time "getting things done"? Of course not. How do we know this? Because even simply considering the eventuality of death (which we all must face) boils everything down to what is really important: love, enjoyment, and generally living life to the fullest. (This is not to say that there is not also a time for hard work; it is just to say that if we exclude the enjoyment of life and the moment, we end up missing the point. And, incidentally, since everything's connected, the quality of our work will also suffer.)

RELAXATION

Relaxation goes hand in hand with enjoyment. Only when we relax fully can we love fully and passionately. Relaxation is also a prerequisite to receptivity, which (as you will see below) is a necessity when it comes to love, intimacy, and fully activating the romance key.

What's more, when we're in a relationship, we must relax in order to be able to enjoy spending time with our partner. And when we're not in a relationship but would like to be, we must relax in order to be in the energetic flow (and state of mind) that will attract one.

RECEPTIVITY

In the I Ching, the area associated with the romance key is sometimes called "receptive earth." And receptivity is really the crux of the matter.

To illustrate, imagine:

- A flower opening up to receive sunlight
- Arms opening up to enfold a loved one
- Soil receiving seeds and rain before wildflowers blossom forth
- A bed with the covers turned down
- A candlelit table for two, set and ready for a sumptuous feast
- An ear to listen and a shoulder to cry on
- Exhaling fully before inhaling a delicious scent

We all give and receive in hundreds of ways every day. But the balance gets thrown off and our receptivity suffers when we focus on "doing" to the exclusion of "being." Even though most of us have a lot of responsibilities and tasks we want to complete, we must balance all this "doing" with moments of simply "being" so that we can be receptive and open to our partners, to our potential partners, or to romance in general.

This is why the serenity key (key #1) actually supports the romance key in a powerful way—it's a holistic science, remember? So if you feel that your romance key is suffering because you spend an average day doing-doing-doing and going-going-going, you might want to revisit chapter 1.

Sometimes we do just fine being serene by ourselves (as we discussed with the serenity key), but when it comes to our partner or potential partners, we feel we have to entertain them or "keep them happy" rather than simply relax and spend time together. Underneath this feeling there is a panic that if we just relax and let ourselves off the hook, the other person will not love us or find us interesting. Underneath this feeling is a fear of being unloved, and this fear blocks our receptivity and undermines our efforts to strike a harmonious balance.

In a situation like this, it is important that we get in touch with the infinite love that comes from the Mother Goddess/ earth so that we know we are loved as a matter of course: that there is no need to force or convince anyone to love us, because we are already infinitely loved and infinitely lovable.

Another aspect of receptivity is *allowing*. Love is everywhere and all around us. When we let our defenses down and simply allow it, not only do we activate the romance key, but—since love is the fabric of the universe—we open up to receiving all other sorts of blessings as well, including blessings related to wealth and success.

GIVING AND RECEIVING LOVE

Nothing is more important than giving and receiving love—nothing. Giving and receiving love are the most satisfying, most gratifying, and most delicious pastimes we could possibly engage in. No one ever looked back on his life and said, "If only I had spent less time and energy giving and receiving love."

And even though it can seem tricky sometimes (many of us go through times when we feel unlovable, and we all know how common it is to have relationship issues), in truth it is the simplest thing in the world, because we are all manifestations of the Divine, and another word for the Divine is, simply, love. In other words, we are love made manifest.

Then why all the drama? And why all the looking in the mirror and inwardly saying negative things about ourselves?

Because this current life experience in which we find ourselves is characterized by the illusion of separation, and another way to say "the illusion of separation" is simply "the human ego."

I do not profess to know why this is so, but I do profess to have observed that it is so. I have also observed that this particular life experience is beautiful and magical exactly as it is, and that if it weren't for the illusion of separation, I wouldn't be able to see it from the precise, breathtaking viewpoint that I now hold.

It is like we are all the same light reflected through our own unique prismatic forms so that we can, for a moment, marvel at the beauty of our magnificence and observe the many forms this magnificence can take.

You might say that temporarily forgetting that we are one with divine light is all part of the spiraling, sparkling, self-realizing experience. But when we remember as much as we can and celebrate the light as it shines through everyone (including us), and trust that there is more than enough love for us and everyone else, we enjoy life more and we experience the full flowering of the romance key.

To do so, we must breathe deeply, relax fully, and allow our hearts to open like flowers in the sun. Is it scary? Yes, because feeling our feelings can hurt, and loving fully and bravely can result in an insatiable, constant, and ever-so-sweet feeling of yearning. Still, it's worth it to push past the fear in order to live with an open heart. After all, what other way would you want to live?

BEAUTY

By "beauty" I do not mean the beauty department in the drugstore. Nor do I mean the standard of beauty as defined by fashion magazines.

I mean the beauty that goes hand in hand with love: the beauty that we see when we look at someone we love, or the beauty that we hear when we listen to that loved one's voice.

I also mean the beauty that we see when we look into our own eyes in the mirror with love and acceptance. And I mean the beauty that we feel in our hearts when we consider our own uniqueness and magnificence.

And, finally, I mean the beauty that we see in the world around us when we know that it is simply a reflection of the Divine, of the God/dess, and of love.

When we are tuned in to the energy of beauty (as defined above), we naturally spread beauty everywhere we go, whether we're creating art, decorating our homes, adorning or pampering our bodies, or simply leaving feelings of love and acceptance in our wake. When nourished by this deep and true sense of beauty, all of these acts are equally imbued with love, and all of them have the power to transform negativity into positivity and discord into harmony.

Practice: BEAUTY TUNE-IN

Take some deep breaths and relax. Now, no matter where you are, notice the beauty that surrounds you: the steam rising from your coffee, the sunlight dancing through the window, the languorous softness of your sleeping cat, the vibrant color of your shirt.

COMFORT WITH SEXUALITY

Our sexuality is a powerful magical force. When we own our sexuality and feel comfortable with our sexuality, we are tremendously powerful and potent. We have good boundaries and feel able to shape our lives according to our desires. When another person or group owns our sexuality or siphons off a part of it for their own personal use, their ego/ego objectives/group objectives become empowered and our spiritual power seemingly becomes diminished. Unfortunately, this happens frequently in our culture to people of all genders and sexual orientations. Fortunately, once we become conscious of it, we can take our power back.

Let's become conscious of it now by taking a look at ways that people and groups may attempt to steal all or part of our sexual power for their personal use.

Historically/Culturally. One only has to look at the major world religions to see examples of organizations siphoning off sexual power for their own gain. As we speak, the Catholic Church says that birth control is a sin, causing child after child to be born into poverty (each of whom they intend to be raised as a loyal and alms-paying member of the church). There was a time when Christianity criminalized powerful or attractive females (and sometimes the men who loved them), literally drowning them, burning them, and torturing them to death. Even today, many Christian and Muslim churches the world over place sanctions on sexuality meant to shame us out of the pure enjoyment and freedom that is our birthright. (For example, many church groups in the United States are working to prevent same-sex marriage, spewing out the confused message that certain varieties of love and sexuality are bad, while others are acceptable.)

In some cases, the leaders of whole countries criminalize and violently punish certain types of completely peaceful sexual acts.

And then there is the conditioning we receive from corporations who appear to believe it is in their best interest to uphold an impossible standard of what it means to be sexy—and then convince us that, since we don't measure up to that standard, we must fork over energy in the form of money so that (perhaps! one day!) we may be as desirable as any given runway model (many of whom in real life feel hopelessly undesirable as well).

In Childhood/Adolescence. With the above historical/cultural conditions in place—even if we have very sexually free and open-minded parents—many of us still grow up with the idea that sexuality is somehow naughty, shameful, and generally bad. And between movies, TV, and the Internet, we do not escape the social hypnotism that as soon as we hit puberty (another shame-infused concept), we must hope that we are sexy enough to attract admiration rather than disgust.

Unfortunately, all the power madness and resulting confusion surrounding sexuality sometimes leads adults to sexually abuse children, which is one more way our sexual power can be temporarily commandeered.

In Young Adulthood. In our late teens and early to mid-twenties, many of us feel that it is our sole purpose to be sexy and attractive to others. This leads to all sorts of confusion and leaves us open to those who would like to suck our sexual energy, including bosses, coworkers, "love" interests, and of course corporations and advertising firms.

Because of the shame we may have absorbed about our sexuality, during this highly charged sexual time, we may begin to feel especially shameful and turn to a religion or group that affirms the shame we already feel.

One way I've noticed our culture tends to trick males of this age group out of the fullness of their sexual power is to lead them to feel that their sexuality should be (or is) predatory or evil rather than mutually respectful, loving, and free.

One way I've noticed that females of this age group can be tricked out of their sexual power is to set them at odds with each other, as if there is only so much appreciation and love to go around.

In Middle and Old Age. There is also this idea floating around that once we're "too old," we no longer have the right to be sexual or feel attractive. And, unfortunately, because of the strange love/hate relationship our culture has with sexuality, this leads many to fear that once one becomes "too old," he/she is no longer a valuable person who is deserving of love, which of course couldn't be further from the truth.

Okay, it wasn't pretty, but we got through it. It's my hope that, as you read through the above section, you became conscious of some formerly unconscious patterns so that you could proactively choose to believe something much truer: that you are beautiful, that you deserve an infinite amount of love, and that your sexuality is perfect and divine exactly as it is.

It should be noted that this is often an ongoing pursuit but that once we're armed with the truth—and as we work with the suggestions here—the ideas and methods designed to capture our power no longer have the same sort of hold over us.

GROUNDING

When we are in touch with our senses, relaxed, receptive, and in possession of the fullness of our sexual power, it follows that we are grounded. In other words, we feel safe, content, calm, empowered, and nourished by our connections with our loved ones and our oneness with the planet beneath our feet.

Romance Key-Related Situations

Life situations and intentions that are related to the romance key include:

- Opening the heart to loving and being loved
- Dating
- Moving in with a partner
- Marriage
- Sex and intimacy
- Self-beautification
- Beautification of the home
- Engaging in sensual pleasures such as food, wine, music, and delicious scents
- Vacations
- Massages and self-pampering
- Generally enjoying life
- Feeling supported and loved
- Being awake to the beauty in ourselves and others

Romance Key Affirmations

I love everyone, and everyone loves me.

I am loved and lovable.

I relax deeply and receive fully.

I am sexual, sensual, beautiful, and free to be me.

I revel in my senses and surrender to the fullness of the moment.

I am totally open and receptive to love.

I am totally open and receptive to blessings of all varieties.

I relax, listen, and allow.

It is safe to give and receive love.

I open my heart to love.

I welcome life's pleasures.

The Alchemy of Romance

The romance key is unique in the way it infuses our entire life experience with feelings of sweetness, comfort, and meaning. (This is true whether we desire to be in a romantic relationship or not.) Perhaps this is because beauty is what gives life its luster, and giving and receiving love are the most precious and gratifying of all endeavors.

In addition to helping us experience the love relationship that we most desire, the information in this chapter—when put to proper use—will help us fall even more deeply in love with ourselves, others, and life itself.

Please note that because intimacy and relaxation are so powerfully associated with the bedroom, your bedroom might be considered a secondary romance area in your home whether or not it falls into the romance area according to your home's magical floor plan. Please also note that if it's a viable option, the romance area is an excellent place for your bedroom.

Romance Key Symbols

THE NUMBER TWO

If it weren't for nighttime, there would be no point to the word *daytime*, just as if there were no emptiness, the word *form* would be meaningless. The appearance of duality, then, is what allows us to perceive and make sense of the world as we know it.

And, just like the romance key itself, the number two signifies the balance of polarities and the appreciation of the sensory world, as well as receptivity and primordial feminine energy.

Here are some ideas for activating the romance key with the number two:

- If you place one thing in your bedroom or the romance area of your home, consider placing two things, coupled and chosen in ways that are evocative of romance: two chairs (or two places to sit, as with a love seat), two nightstands, two statues, two lamps, two pictures (or one picture depicting two things), etc.

- Empower two hearts made of rose quartz with the energy of romance by conjuring up exactly the romantic feelings you'd like to experience and directing these feelings into the crystals. Place them in your bedroom or the romance area of your home.

- Create a love-drawing charm by placing two lodestones in a red flannel bag along with a pinch of vervain and five red rose petals. Keep it close to you during the day or sleep with it under your pillow.

ROMANTIC IMAGERY

Naturally, if an image evokes the feelings you'd like to experience in the romance department, it will be a powerful tool for enhancing the romance key in your life. For example, this might be a painting or statue of a couple embracing, dancing, or holding hands. (In this case, it will be especially important to take a good look at both members of the couple to make sure they appear happy and interested in the relationship.) Or it might be a painting of a café in Paris or a silver charm etched with two intertwining roses (if those are things you're into).

Here are some ideas for activating the romance key with romantic imagery:

- Display it in your bedroom or the romance area of your home.

- Employ it in the construction of a charm that you can carry with you.

- Wear it (such as on a T-shirt or a belt buckle).

- Have it tattooed onto your body.

EXPANSES OF EARTH

As I mentioned above, many I Ching translations use the words "receptive earth" to denote the energies associated with the romance key.

Here are some ideas for activating the romance key with them:

- Plant and tend a flower garden.

- Display one or more pictures or paintings of expanses of fertile earth (preferably containing red or pink flowers).

- Recline in a flat, expansive area in nature such as a meadow or beach (alone or with a partner).

- Take a walk or a hike in nature on a pleasant late summer day (alone or with a partner).

HEARTS

More than any other symbol, hearts are synonymous with romance and love. As such, they powerfully evoke the energies associated with the romance key. Notice that the cleft at the top is evocative of receptivity, softness, balance, and the number two, while the point at the bottom indicates fiery passion and the focused power that occurs when two people are aligned in mutually supportive oneness.

Here are some ideas for activating the romance key with them:

- If you're into the idea, decorate with hearts in the romance area of your home.

- On a Friday during the waxing moon, empower a heart-shaped pendant with your romantic intentions, then wear it.

- Wear clothing that depicts hearts.

- Place two rose quartz hearts in the romance area of your home.

- Create a romance charm by cutting two equally sized hearts out of red or pink felt. Sew them together with golden thread and place between your mattress and box spring.

FLOWERS

Certainly for thousands of years, but probably for as long as there have been humans, flowers have been associated with the essences of romance and beauty. And how could they not be? One only has to consciously gaze at one to see that they evoke receptivity, divine love, beauty for beauty's sake, heart opening, passion, joy, and all the spinning, swirling, sweep-you-off-your-feet brilliance associated with this alchemical key.

It's no wonder, then, that the gift of flowers is known by folks of all spiritual persuasions for its miraculous ability to evoke romantic feelings in the recipient.

Here are some ideas for activating the romance key with them:

- Bring fresh flowers into your space (and perhaps into the romance area of your home).

- Plant blossoming plants in outdoor areas.

- Place rose petals in your bathwater.

- Flavor your drinking water with rose water.

- Scent your home with floral essential oils such as ylang ylang, jasmine, neroli, or rose.

- Anoint yourself with perfume made from floral essential oils.

- Decorate with floral imagery in the romance area of your home (especially in romance colors—see page 167).

Romance Key Deities

Divinities that are associated with romantic love, beauty, receptivity, and sensuality are especially in alignment with this key. Below you'll find some that fall into these categories. To help activate and heal your relationship with this key, you might strike up a relationship with any or all of them. You might also wear jewelry depicting one of them or display one or more of them on your altar.

Please note that I do not suggest bringing lone figures (even of love goddesses) into your bedroom or the romance area of your home, as they can throw off the ideal balance of polarities that is associated with this life area. Instead, if you want to display divinities in either of these areas, I suggest bringing in a pair of deities that represent the type of romantic relationship you'd like to experience. Unfortunately, at this point in the evolution of our culture, imagery of same-sex deities may be a little more difficult to find, but you might create a painting or statue yourself, enlist an artist's help, or get creative by placing two statues or paintings together evocatively. Here are some ideas for deity couples for various types of relationships:

- For male/female relationships, consider Krishna and Radha or Buddha with his consort.

- For male/male relationships, consider Apollo and Hyacinth, Odin and Loki, or Dionysus and Adonis.

- For female/female relationships, consider Artemis, Diana, Isis, or Ishtar in any combination or with a female consort.

That being said, regardless of your sexual orientation, feel free to call on any of the deities below (even the single ones!) for help with activating the romance key in your life.

HATHOR

The Egyptian deity Hathor embodies all the energies associated with this area: love, beauty, receptivity, sensuality, and the Great Mother Goddess.

VENUS AND APHRODITE

These Roman and Greek love goddess incarnations have intertwined over the centuries to become one and the same. Venus/Aphrodite is the essence of feminine sexuality, sensuality, beauty, and romantic love.

KRISHNA AND RADHA

Krishna and Radha, the divine lovers in the Hindu tradition, represent romance, passion, sensuality, divine love, and balanced duality.

BUDDHA AND CONSORT

For those of you who love your Buddha statues and imagery, the Buddha with his consort can be a lovely, sexy variation on the theme for your romance area.

FREYA

When you're ready to add a little spiciness, passion, and sexual power into the mix, or when sexual healing is a consideration, you might call on Freya for help. In addition to being a goddess of love and beauty, she also possesses a fierceness and an empowered confidence that can help us own our sexuality and experience pleasure as a matter of course.

Romance Key Animals

Like deities, each animal carries its own unique qualities and helpful energy. To activate the romance key in your life, you can work with the animals below through meditation, prayer, altars, or imagery in your home, on your altar, or on your person (as in jewelry or tattoos).

BUTTERFLIES

In the same way that the energies associated with the serenity key prepare us for experiencing ideal romance, before a butterfly becomes a butterfly, he or she goes inward and becomes very still. Then he or she bursts forth in colorful beauty like a flower with wings, just as our hearts do when the romance key is activated and flowing in our life. This is why two butterflies together are a potent symbol of relationship harmony.

MANDARIN DUCKS

Traditionally in China, because mandarin ducks mate for life and because they are often seen together in pairs, they are seen as a potent symbol of marital bliss.

DOVES

Doves also mate for life, and—similar to mandarin ducks in the East—doves are often seen as symbols of divine love as experienced through romantic relationships.

Romance Key Colors

To activate or enhance the romance key in your life, you might work with any or all of the following colors, perhaps in one or more of the following ways:

- Wear one or more of them.

- Obtain two candles in one of the colors. Charge them with a romance-related intention, place them side by side in your romance area or bedroom, and light. Allow them to melt together as they eventually burn all the way down.

- Decorate with one or more of the colors in any combination in the romance area of your home.

  Reds: Red symbolizes passion and romantic love.

  Whites and Creams: In this context, whites and creams symbolize purity and the clarity of thought that allows us to make sound decisions in the romance department.

  Pinks: Because red is the fire element and whites/creams are the metal element, pink is a very melty color— red fire (passion) warming, melting, and tempering precise metal (purity and clarity of thought). The result is a very sweet, warm, fuzzy, romantic color.

Oranges, Yellows, Beiges, Tans, and Browns: In feng shui, all of these colors fall into the earthy realm (although orange also contains a bit of fire). This means that they will add sensuality, grounding, and receptivity, although when employed alone (without pinks or reds), you might end up craving a bit more sweetness than passion. Consequently, I consider them secondary relationship colors, while reds, pinks, and whites/creams are primary relationship colors.

Romance Key Herbs

ROSE

Almost nothing (other than a heart) says "romantic love" like a rose, especially a red, pink, or white one (see above for color connotations). If you tune in to the personality of a rose, you will find that it is none other than the actual energy of love made manifest in the visible or tangible world. As such, it has a very pure and positive vibration. In fact, many say that it has the most positive vibration of any living thing.

Try:

- Strewing rose petals over the top of your bed to empower it with the energy of romance (leave for at least twelve hours)

- Misting your home with rose water
- Planting roses in your yard
- Bringing fresh roses into your home
- Adding rose petals to your bath

HIBISCUS

The bright and passionate nature of the hibiscus blossom is also powerfully aligned with romance, especially the sensual side of it.

Try:

- Planting hibiscus in your yard
- Adding a bit of hibiscus tea and a bit of pomegranate juice to a glass (or two!) of pink champagne to create a passion potion

DAMIANA

Damiana is the "go to" herb for many herbalists and magical practitioners when it comes to spicing up the love life and igniting passion.

Try:

- Stuffing a small red flannel bag with dried damiana and two garnets, and tying it around the doorknob on your bedroom door.
- Empowering a small bowl of dried damiana with the intention to manifest a sensual awakening or a passionate love affair and sprinkling it along the pathway leading up to your front door.

Romance Key Crystals

To receive the romance key–enhancing benefits of any of the crystals below, wear one of them, carry a pair of them, or place a pair of them in the romance area of your home. You may also empower them with any of the romance key affirmations that appear earlier in this chapter.

ROSE QUARTZ

This pink crystal has a heart-opening, heart-soothing softness that helps heal potential romance-blocking issues and draws warm, fuzzy feelings and relationships into our life experience.

GARNET

Like the romance key itself, garnet is sensual, earthy, and packs a passionate punch. It helps us heal sexual issues, helps get us into our bodies and out of our heads, and encourages sexual freedom.

LEPIDOLITE

Lepidolite is one of my favorites for many reasons, not the least of which is because I was wearing it over my heart when I first met my partner over twelve years ago (and we have been nearly inseparable ever since). Like a butterfly or a glass of pink champagne, it has a sparkly, joyful, magical, heart-opening quality and can help us get into the energy of our most ideal romance before it even arrives (and once this happens, it will only be a matter of time before it does)!

Romance Key Master Ritual

As I alluded to above, the serenity key supports the romance key in a powerful way. So on many occasions when it seems like your romance key could use help, it might actually be the serenity key that needs the most attention.

However, if after reading through this entire book once, you determine that the romance key is the key that could use the most help in your life right now, performing the following ritual will activate and calibrate this key for you in an ideal way.

Provided you've sufficiently tended to your serenity key, you can also perform this ritual anytime that you feel your romance key could use a serious boost.

Because the art of bliss is a holistic science, not only will your romance key benefit from this ritual, but every other life key will benefit as well.

INGREDIENTS

2 sticks vanilla incense

2 red roses

2 pink candles

1 pinch dried damiana

A bottle of cheap red wine (or any red wine you feel comfortable using)

2 small lepidolites, cleansed in cold water and white sage smoke

A delicious chocolate bar

A lighter or matches

On a Friday during a waxing moon, when the moon is visible in the night sky, draw a bath. Light the two pink candles and two sticks of vanilla incense near the bath. Add the entire bottle of red wine, the petals of the roses, and the pinch of damiana to the bathwater.

Hold your hands over the water and say:

> Goddesses of love—Hathor, Venus,
>> and Aphrodite—I call on you!
>
> Infuse this water with your beautiful energy.
>
> Fill me up with the vibrations of
>> passion, romance, and love.
>
> Beautiful goddesses, I thank you!

Soak for at least forty-five minutes, drinking water as necessary to stay hydrated.

Get out, dry off, throw on some sort of loose, comfortable, beautiful clothing (if necessary), and take the lepidolites outside. Hold them up to the light of the moon and say:

> Goddesses of love—Hathor, Venus,
>> and Aphrodite—I call on you!
>
> Please infuse these crystals with the
>> magnetic, swirly, sparkly vibration of
>> open-hearted love and divine passion.
>
> With your help and the help of these
>> crystals, may I become an irresistible
>> love-drawing charm in and of myself.
>
> May I experience divine romance that is
>> perfectly suited to me in every way.

May my love situation shift and change
    according to what is in alignment with
    my truest and most beautiful good.
While my healthy boundaries stay
    strong, may I be totally open and
    receptive to ideal experiences relating
    to beauty, passion, and love.
Thank you, thank you, thank you.
Blessed be! And so it is.

To internalize the energies and seal the deal, slowly and sensuously eat the chocolate. (If you're allergic or don't like chocolate, substitute another sensually delicious treat such as cherries or coconut milk ice cream.)

In the days and weeks ahead, keep the lepidolites near your heart. (You might want to tie them into a piece of cloth and safety-pin them to the inside of your clothes. If this isn't possible with your wardrobe, just keep them somewhere on your person.) Once you feel you've sufficiently drawn in the intended energies, place them on your altar as a reminder and a symbol of sensuality, passion, and divine romance.

6 Radiance

It's the middle of summer. The sun is in the middle of the bright, cloudless sky, and it beats down on you as you recline languidly in the searing desert sand. As the sun spreads its vibrant golden-white light across the planet, you suddenly become exceptionally aware that it is the center of the entire solar system and that everything expands outward from it, relates to it, and revolves around it. Still, despite the fact that its scope is so broad, you realize that its power resides also in your heart. You feel the sun's radiance expanding outward from your heart, warming and giving life to your body and manifesting as a beautiful glow that catches the eyes and hearts of everyone you come into contact with, and even others whom you've never even met. You recognize that it is your divine nature to shine like the sun and to emanate divine light for everyone to see, enjoy, and be nourished by.

> **This is the alchemical essence**
> **of life key #6: radiance.**

If the energies associated with this life key are flowing harmoniously, the following statements will be true for you (and the more ideal the flow, the truer they will be):

- I enjoy sharing my uniqueness and unique gifts with the world.

- I express my talents in ways that nourish both me and others.

- I feel known for the things I'd like to be known for.

- I feel seen in the ways I'd like to be seen.

- I feel my projects and endeavors are steadily gaining recognition or are already receiving the attention they deserve.

- In the right situation, I enjoy being in the limelight.

- I am comfortable expressing my authentic self.

- I like to be noticed and appreciated.

- I receive compliments graciously.

- I like telling stories about myself and my life.

- I laugh easily in public and when I'm spending time with friends.

- I feel like people "get" me.

- I feel comfortable talking about my strengths.

- I feel comfortable saying positive things about my projects and endeavors.

- I feel confident that people enjoy spending time with me.

- I like spending time with others.

- I easily attract like-minded friends and acquaintances.

- When it's the right situation, I look forward to social gatherings and events.

- I feel good about my appearance.

- I feel good about my wardrobe.

- I like looking in the mirror, and I enjoy getting ready to go out.

- I know that in at least one arena (and maybe more), I am a genius.

Qualities Associated with the Radiance Key

The following descriptions are designed to help you determine how well the radiance key is already flowing in your life, and also to begin creating subtle shifts that will prepare you to more fully activate it. As you read, be sure not to judge or berate yourself if these qualities don't perfectly match your current life experience. Instead, relax, perform any or all of the suggested exercises (as you feel moved), and allow the descriptions to infuse your awareness with the qualities they represent.

SHARING YOUR GIFTS/SHINING YOUR LIGHT

Some of us have learned that, in the name of humility or out of respect for others, we're supposed to hide our light and diminish our talents in the eyes of the world. Well, I would like to tell you that nothing could be further from the truth. We are fountains of divine light, and the more we allow this light to shine, the happier we are, and the more beauty, healing, joy, and inspiration we bring into the world.

To illustrate, think of all the people who have ever inspired you or healed you or helped you in any way—whether you know them personally or you only know them through their work. Now imagine that those people all went back in time and decided to hide their light and unique talents from the world. Consider what a cold, dark place your world would become because of their decision to do so.

When we allow our gifts and light to shine, we feel better because we are in our natural state and we are in our divine flow. We feel that we are making a positive difference in a way that only we can, and we feel that we are interacting with the world—and the world is interacting with us—in a deeply satisfying and mutually beneficial way.

Practice: APPRECIATING YOUR RADIANCE KEY HEROES

To change your paradigm so that you can begin to feel comfortable sharing your light generously with the world, take a moment to appreciate those people who have enhanced your life by sharing *their* light. Make a list of about twenty or so. My list would include Gandhi, Paul Simon, Lou Reed, Joni Mitchell, Doreen Virtue, Denise Linn, Louise Hay, Scott Cun-

ningham, my boyfriend Ted, and my best friend Sedona. Then
note some of the qualities each person has shared with you
and the world. Feel gratitude for the courage they have shown
in doing so.

CONFIDENCE

I suspect that even the most seemingly confident people
harbor secret insecurities and have days when they'd rather
stay home and hide away from the world. Still, when we're
in alignment with the radiance key, our confidence generally
wins out over our moments of low self-esteem. Most days
we look in the mirror and feel proud, not just of the way
we look but also of who we are and what we do. We don't
worry about what to say or not say, because we don't have
anything to prove or conceal. Are we a little bit odd? Sure!
Who isn't? But our idiosyncrasies are something to embrace
or get a kick out of rather than something to be ashamed of.

EXPANSIVENESS

In the same way that sunlight expands outward across the
solar system or fireworks start as condensed explosions and
then reach brilliantly across the sky, when we're in alignment
with the radiance key, we continually expand our sphere
of influence and allow ourselves to be seen and known to
greater and greater degrees. We're receptive to opportunities,
and when they knock, we answer the door. Through continually making space for the ever-expanding light to shine
through us to greater and greater degrees, we create our own
luck and follow the natural course of our personal success.

VISIBILITY

The old movie cliché "I can see it now: my name in lights!" is a visualization and affirmation of an activated and flowing radiance key. Even the term *star* (when it means "celebrity") is a clear reference to the bright, radiant, visible light aligned with this key. While not all of us want to be stars of the stage or silver screen, on some level all of us want to be known and seen for our unique gifts: those magical things that we are best at and love doing.

It's important to note that this is true for everyone. It is not a weakness or something to be ashamed of; it is a natural aspect of being a human. We are social creatures, and we want to be seen and recognized in a positive light.

You might think of it like this: we are a generous species. Our uniqueness and special talents are wonderful gifts, and it is our heart's desire to lovingly bestow them upon the world. Then, like any gift giver, we want to know that the recipient of our gifts (the world) noticed them, noticed us, and appreciated both.

ATTRACTIVENESS

A well-lit front door at night feels welcoming and inviting. A candlelit table beckons diners to approach. And when we're lit up from within by that radiance key charm, we feel attractive: we attract attention and admiration in a powerful way. You know when you meet or see someone whom you have a hard time looking away from—not necessarily because they're classically beautiful or look like a picture in a fashion magazine, but because of a certain indefinable *something*? That something is the radiance key attracting your eye (and interest) like a sparkling jewel.

FAME

The radiance key is closely associated with the energy of fame, whether it's in larger circles (whole countries or the world) or smaller circles (certain industries, artistic genres, schools, or organizations).

As you've probably noticed, many people we call "famous" or even just "popular" don't appear to be exceptionally balanced, healthy, or happy (though some of them are). To look at this from an alchemical perspective, consider fire. It warms us, nourishes us, and keeps us alive. But left unchecked, while it might burn beautifully while it lasts, it ends up leaving us dried up, burned out, out of control, or totally destroyed. (Consider Jimi Hendrix living the last years of his short life in a wildfire of fame, fueled by his literally burning guitar.)

This is why it's especially important to make sure the radiance key is well aspected by the other keys, especially the life path key (which, remember, possesses the essence of water and the ocean). In fact, ideally, the life path key and the radiance key work in harmony to keep us balanced with the way we express our uniqueness and share our gifts with the world.

In other words, how can we share our uniqueness and authenticity with the world (in other words, activate the radiance key) if we don't first get in touch with it on our own (by activating the life path key)? Conversely, how can our deep inner truth (life path key) really feel satisfying to us if we don't get to share it with the world (radiance key)?

Or you might think of it this way: most living things need a certain balance of sunlight and water to thrive.

REPUTATION

In the I Ching, the radiance key is aligned with the term *clinging fire*, and in traditional feng shui it's said that our reputation "clings to us like fire," meaning once we've acquired a certain type of recognition or notoriety, it's difficult to shake. Still, when the radiance key is activated and flowing—and when it's tempered with a balanced and activated life path key—there is no way that we will not eventually come into a positive relationship with the way that others see us. Of course, we will never know for sure what they are thinking (nor should we lose sleep over it), but any aspects of our reputation that affect our overall happiness and bliss will come into an ideal sort of alignment and flow.

Practice:

HOW WOULD YOU LIKE TO BE KNOWN AND SEEN?

Without thinking too much about it, write answers to the following questions:

1. In my heart of hearts, in what ways would I like to be known and seen by others?

2. What skills/activities/qualities would I like to be known and seen for?

3. Who are some people who are known and seen in ways that I would like to be known and seen?

4. What visible, perceptible qualities in others do I admire?

5. What message do I want to send to the world?

6. What concrete steps can I take to come more deeply into alignment with my highest vision for how I would like to be known and seen?

LAUGHTER

In the same way fire can transmute dead, brittle wood into vibrant heat and light, laughter can transmute sadness, irony, and despair into happiness and joy. What's more, true laughter is expansive. It opens us up and connects us with others. When our radiance key is flowing, our heart is open and our belly is relaxed so that true, deep laughter expands outward from our heart and upward from our gut. That's why you can help activate the radiance key by:

- Watching a funny movie or comedy show

- Being silly with your friends or family

- Doing laughter yoga (forcing laughter for a set amount of time until it begins to feel natural and real—see chapter 4)

- Having a sense of humor about yourself and your life

Radiance Key-Related Situations

Life situations and intentions that are related to the radiance key include:

- Starting a new career or business venture
- Parties and gatherings
- Marketing and publicity
- Meeting new people and making new friends
- Interviews, meetings, and presentations
- Public speaking
- Shows of all kinds (art, music, theater, etc.)
- Positive attention
- Charm and attractiveness
- Being in the limelight
- Confidence in social situations
- Spending time with others
- Being in a leadership role
- Generally being recognized in whatever ways you'd most like to be recognized

Radiance Key Affirmations

I am a fountain of divine radiance.

Everything I touch is a raging success.

I am a channel of divine light.

I shine like the sun.

My divine radiance is now expanding.

I am on fire with success.

I am a brightly shining star.

I am awake to my own brilliance.

I bless the world with my beautiful light.

My heart is brighter than the sun.

I love everyone, and everyone loves me.

The Alchemy of Radiance

The alchemy of radiance is the alchemy of sunlight: that blinding glow that stretches over our world, illuminating, warming, and uniting us all. But it's also within you; if your unique personality were a jewel, this radiance would be the thing that lights you up from the inside so that you naturally emanate joy and warmth, and so that your presence can help beautify and illuminate the world.

Radiance Key Symbols

THE NUMBER NINE

Like all odd numbers, three is dynamic and lively, yet it's also harmoniously balanced. Three times three is nine: a magical number that radiates out in all directions, sparkling and spreading through the kaleidoscopic interplay of numbers in a irresistibly mysterious way. With nine life keys and nine corresponding life areas, nine is the mystical spark that spreads throughout all life areas, infusing it with form, mean-ing, dynamism, and life.

According to the authors of *Angel Numbers*, Doreen Vir-tue and Lynnette Brown, the number nine means that "your divine life purpose involves the giving of service through your natural talents, passions, and interests"—the radiance key in a nutshell.

Here are some ideas for activating the radiance key with the number nine:

- Buy or create artwork depicting nine red stars and place it in the radiance area of the home.

- Place nine plants in nine red pots in the radiance area of the home.

- Create a radiance charm by collecting nine naturally shed feathers and tying them together with red string in an attractive and interesting way. Weave or tie in nine small bells or beads as well, and hang it in a window in the radiance area of your home or business.

- While standing in the radiance area of your home, hold your hands up just below shoulder level, palms out. Flick your fingers outward like small explosions. Repeat nine times as you visualize/imagine/feel the type of radiance-related success you desire and say any of the affirmations from earlier in this chapter, repeating the affirmation once for each time you flick your fingers.

REPRESENTATIONS OF HOW YOU'D
LIKE TO BE SEEN OR KNOWN

Locating, identifying, or creating and then surrounding yourself with clear representations of exactly how you'd like to be seen or known in the world is a powerful way to begin to manifest your radiance-related goals.

Here are some ideas for activating the radiance key with them:

- Remember your radiance key heroes from earlier in this chapter? Or perhaps there are others you may not have listed: for example, maybe you'd like your writing to be respected like Jack Kerouac's or your acting to be celebrated like Meryl Streep's. If you like the idea of displaying pictures or representations of your radiance key heroes in your home, place them in your radiance area to help attune yourself to their vibration and manifest similar success. (Although you will want to be careful with this. For example, if you've ever had a drug problem, it probably won't be a good idea to live with a poster of Jim Morrison in your space.) You might also consider placing radiance key hero imagery as the wallpaper on your computer or phone.

- Place representations of past successes in your radiance area. For example, if you directed a play that had critical success

and you'd like to direct more like that,
you might frame the poster for the play
or a picture of you with the cast and place
it in the radiance area of your home.

- If you create any sort of art or craft
and you'd like to be known for it, you
might display pieces of your work in
the radiance area of your home.

- If your artwork or business has received
a favorable review in the paper or in a
magazine, you might frame it and hang it in
the radiance area of your home or business.

- If you have a diploma, certificate, or award that
you're particularly proud of and would like
to display, the radiance area of your home or
business would be an excellent place to do it.

STARS, SUNS, AND OTHER RADIAL SHAPES

Stars are such a powerful representation of fame. You see them everywhere in Hollywood, and the word *star* is even used in place of the word *celebrity*. Perhaps this is because you can see starlight from incomprehensible distances or because starlight moves out in all directions or because stars are often (like our sun) the centers of solar systems around which everything in their general vicinity revolves.

By radial shapes, I mean shapes that have branches, arms, or rays that reach out from the center, such as symmetrical flower shapes. Radial shapes, like star and sun shapes, are, well, *radiant*.

Here are some ideas for activating the radiance key with them:

- Display it in the radiance area of your home.

- Incorporate it into clothing, jewelry, or tattoos.

- Attractively paint a decorative wooden five-pointed star (available at many craft stores) and write, paint, or stencil your name in the middle. Attach it to the outside of your bedroom door to remind yourself that you are a star. Consider adding glitter.

- Envision a huge golden sunshine around your entire body and aura, allowing you to radiate your brilliant light out into the world for everyone to see and enjoy.

- Envision a glowing, white-hot sunshine or five-pointed star at your sternum, in the same vicinity as your heart.

TRIANGLES (AND DIAMONDS, ZIG-ZAG SHAPES, AND DIAGONAL LINES)

Triangles and shapes that incorporate triangles (such as diamonds, zig-zags, and diagonal lines) have a fiery, dynamic, electrical energy that can activate the radiance key in a powerful way.

Here are some ideas for activating the radiance key with them:

- Choose prints or imagery containing any or all of these shapes when decorating the radiance area of your home.

- If you have throw pillows in the radiance area of your home, display them with the points at vertical and horizontal planes (so that they appear as diamonds rather than squares).

- If possible and attractive, display and position items at diagonals in the radiance area of your home.

REPRESENTATIONS OF PEOPLE

The same mysterious spark that causes fires to dance animates all people and fills us with a warm, inviting, social quality. What's more, the radiance key is all about our social interactions and sharing our gifts with other people in the world. As such, representations of people are potent radiance key activators.

For example, when choosing artwork or photos for the radiance area of your home, you might choose pieces that depict people, making sure that any pieces you choose for this area also give you positive feelings associated with achieving your radiance key goals.

REPRESENTATIONS OF ANIMALS

Animal imagery, items that come from animals (such as naturally shed feathers or found seashells), and items that appear to come from animals (such as faux fur, faux leather, faux silk, or animal prints) also have that warm, fiery, visible, social quality associated with the radiance key. (Case in point: rock-star wardrobes!)

Unless they are upcycled or salvaged, I don't suggest obtaining actual animal-derived fabrics such as leather, fur, ivory, or purchased feathers, shells, or bone, as they powerfully hold the energy of pain and suffering in almost all cases.

Here are some ideas for activating the radiance key with them:

- When choosing artwork or photos for the radiance area of your home, choose artwork or photos depicting animals, making sure that the piece also gives you positive feelings associated with achieving your radiance key goals.

- Choose animal prints, faux leather, faux fur, or faux or salvaged silk when decorating the radiance area of your home.

- Wear animal prints, faux leather, faux or salvaged silk, or faux fur.

LIGHTING AND ACTUAL FIRE

As we've seen, the radiance key is all about fire and light, so actual fire and light are naturally potent activators of the radiance key.

Here are some ideas for activating the radiance key with lighting:

- Place red candles (or any candles) in the radiance area of your home and light them on occasion.

- Choose fun or flashy lighting for the radiance area of your home, such as red light bulbs, lava lamps, or twinkle lights.

- Make sure the lighting outside your home or business feels welcoming at night.

PLANTS AND ITEMS MADE OF WOOD

Obviously, although wood is one of the elements in the Chinese five-element system, wood is not the element associated with the radiance key: fire is. But wood is fuel for the fire, so when a fiery element is already present (such as in any of the above symbols), wood can amplify its potency.

Here are some ideas for activating the radiance key with wood:

- Choose wooden elements and accents for the radiance area of your home.

- Add plants to the radiance area of your home.

Radiance Key Deities

Divinities that are associated with fire, light, and radiance are especially in alignment with this key. Below, you'll find some that fall into these categories. To help activate and heal your relationship with this key, you might strike up a relationship with any or all of them. You might also wear jewelry depicting one of them or display one or more of them on your altar.

PELE

A Hawaiian volcano goddess, Pele is aligned with smoldering passion, anger, and all things hot. She can help us stay grounded as our talents erupt in a fountain of heat and light that can be seen and felt for miles around.

BRIGHID

Brighid is a beloved redheaded Celtic goddess associated with fire and the sun. She infuses us with brightness and warmth and helps us be successful in all that we do.

LUGH

A male counterpart to Brighid, Lugh is a Celtic god associated with the sun. He bestows vibrant health, aligns us with bright prospects, and helps us manifest our brightest possible future.

AMERATASU

Ameratasu is a Japanese goddess associated with the sun. In her most famous story, she (as an embodiment of the sun) hides herself away until everyone misses her and she finally returns, once again sharing her warmth and shining her glorious light. For this reason, she's a great ally to call on when—in alignment with our true nature—we want to come out of hiding and begin to generously share our divine light with the world.

Radiance Key Animals

Like deities, each animal carries its own unique qualities and helpful energy. To activate the radiance key in your life, you can work with the animals below through meditation, prayer, altars, or imagery in your home, on your altar, or on your person (as in jewelry or tattoos).

LION

If you're into astrology, you may have noticed that the radiance key and the astrological sign of Leo have a lot in common. Leo's symbol, the lion, is the king of the forest in the same way that the sun is the king of the sky. And, like the sun, he glows and radiates with a searing power. Being the center of attention comes naturally to him, and consciously aligning with his energy can help us feel the same way.

TIGER

In Chinese astrology and symbolism, the tiger is similar to the lion, with his bright showiness and confident stride.

DRAGON

Dragons don't just breathe fire, they embody fire: you might think of a dragon as fire with a conscious awareness. In both Western and Eastern symbolism, dragons are symbols of the most potent form of personal power.

Radiance Key Colors

To activate or enhance the radiance key in your life, you might work with any or all of the following colors, perhaps in one or more of the following ways:

- Wear one or more of them.

- Obtain one candle in one of the colors. Charge it with a radiance-related intention, place it in your radiance area, and light it. Extinguish when necessary and light again when possible until it burns all the way down.

- Decorate with one or more of the colors, in any combination, in the radiance area of your home.

    Reds: Any shade of red is the color related to the fire element and radiance key. It's expansive, visible, cheerful, social, and bright.

    Bright Orange: Like red, bright orange is fiery, expansive, and very noticeable.

    Hot Pink: Also fiery, expansive, and noticeable but with a hint of femininity and sweet sassiness thrown in.

    Please note: Since the wood element feeds the fire element, colors associated with wood might be considered secondary colors associated with this life key. These include blues and greens.

Radiance Key Herbs

CAYENNE

If there is such a thing as an herbal manifestation of fire, cayenne is it. It's hot, bright red, cleansing, and activating.

Try:

- Sprinkling powdered cayenne over a picture of yourself or a representation of your project or aspirations to help manifest your radiance-related goals

- Ingesting cayenne to help internalize the energy of radiance

CINNAMON

Another bright, warming, fiery herb, cinnamon also helps activate the radiance key. Whether it's employed in a culinary, magical, or aromatherapeutic manner (or any combination of the three), it helps us love and approve of ourselves so that we can generously share our gifts with confidence and joy. As if that weren't enough, it magically allows us to receive abundance and wealth for doing the things that make our hearts sing.

Try:

- Burning cinnamon incense
- Diffusing cinnamon essential oil
- Adding cinnamon to your coffee
- Adding cinnamon to your food

- Adding cinnamon to cookie batter and stirring in a clockwise direction as you repeat any of the affirmations from earlier in the chapter nine times. Then, as they bake, put your hands on the outside of the oven door and repeat the affirmation nine more times. When you ingest the cookies, you will be ingesting the energy of the radiance key.

Radiance Key Crystals

To receive the radiance key–enhancing benefits of either of the crystals below, wear or carry one of them or place one of them in the radiance area of your home. You may also empower one or both them with any of the radiance key affirmations from earlier in the chapter.

TIGER'S-EYE

Tiger's-eye can help us know ourselves, focus and magnify our talents, and bravely share our talents with the world. Along with its complex layers and prismatic depth, this crystal has a light that seems to shine from within.

SUNSTONE

Sunstone also appears to emanate its own light, and it has a bright and sunny quality that lifts our spirits and enhances our confidence. Wearing it or carrying it can help us to have fun in social settings and enjoy sharing our unique light with the world.

Radiance Key Master Ritual

As I have mentioned, the radiance key works in harmony with the life path key, and each is necessary to the other in order to experience an ideal balance with regard to knowing who you are and expressing yourself in satisfying ways. So if you feel that your radiance key challenges may, in fact, stem from not being in alignment with your authenticity and deepest inner truth, start by working with the life path key instead of the radiance key.

If, however, after reading through this entire book once, you determine that the radiance key is the key that could use the most help in your life right now, performing the following ritual will activate and calibrate this key for you in an ideal way.

Provided you've sufficiently tended to your life path key, you can also perform this ritual anytime that you feel your radiance key could use a serious boost. Because the art of bliss is a holistic science, not only will your radiance key benefit from this ritual, but every other life key will benefit as well.

It's best to do this ritual on a Sunday or when the moon is in Leo.

INGREDIENTS

1 small orange

1 lemon

A lemon squeezer

A glass for drinking water

⅛ teaspoon cayenne pepper

A fireplace or fire pit

Stuff with which to build a fire

9 cinnamon sticks

Something with which to stir your potion
(possibly a chopstick or a spoon)

Music that inspires you and gives you confidence,
whatever that means to you (you'll know)

To prepare for the ritual, shower or bathe and then dress and groom yourself as if you were going out. As much as possible, think positive thoughts about yourself as you look in the mirror. Wear an outfit that's both comfortable and flattering. In all your fashion choices, lean as far toward flashy as you can.

Using the lemon squeezer, squeeze the orange and lemon juice into the glass. Add the cayenne pepper, and fill the rest of the glass with water. Set aside.

Build a fire. When it's up and going, start the music. With your cayenne-citrus potion and all the rest of your ingredients nearby, stand in a relaxed way in front of the fire and take some deep breaths. Begin to feel yourself merging with the music and the fire, and feel the music and the fire merging with you.

Hold the cinnamon sticks in both hands and say:

> **With this cinnamon, I now summon
> the energy of radiance.**

Throw them in the fire. As they burn, hold the potion toward the fire and say:

> **Fire, please warm this potion with**
> **the energy of radiance.**
> **Fill it with sparkle, fill it with light.**

Become conscious of the potion swirling and pulsating with radiant, fiery light. Then stir it in a clockwise direction as you repeat the following nine times:

> **I am awake to my own radiance, and I**
> **generously share my beauty with the world.**

While standing in front of the fire, drink your potion. Feel yourself ingesting the radiant, fiery energy that it contains.

Close your eyes and feel yourself emanating the beautiful, sparkling light that is your true essence. Slowly, and in a contained way, begin to let this energy move your body in the form of dancing. Stay grounded in your body and in the moment as you let this energy continue to spread throughout your limbs. Dance more and more freely as you consciously and masterfully wield this radiant energy.

Once your dancing comes to a natural conclusion, bring yourself back into a very still and grounded place. Hold your hands in prayer pose and close your eyes. Feel willing to generously shine your light into the world and to enjoy connecting with others in this way.

Take some deep breaths and say:

> I shine like the sun.
> I reign like a queen/king.
> I radiate my beauty and talents
> for all to see and enjoy.
> I love who I am.
> I love what I do.
> I am on fire with my own brilliant light.

7 | Prosperity

It's warm out, yet you feel that early summer breath of cool-
ness that hearkens back to the late springtime rain. White
clouds drift lazily in the bright blue sky. Palm trees rustle in
the wind, and turquoise ocean waves lap serenely at the shore.
You recline comfortably, take a sip of your delicious bever-
age, and consider how amazingly blessed you are: you love
your work and you love your play. You love your family and
friends. You love your home, your transportation, your body,
your wardrobe, and all your many blessings in the seen and
unseen realms. You marvel at the way each blessing enhances
the others, and all yield beautiful, eminently satisfying returns.

This is the alchemical essence of
life key #7: prosperity.

If the energies associated with this life key are flowing harmoniously, the following statements will be true for you (and
the more ideal the flow, the truer they will be):

- Most days I wake up with joy in my heart.

- Most days I wake up looking
forward to my day.

- I often find myself marveling at
how lucky and blessed I am.

- I am exceptionally grateful for
the blessings in my life.

- I am exceptionally grateful for the
people and animals in my life.

- I don't have to look too hard to
find things to be thankful for.

- I know that I am a divine child and that I
deserve to experience wealth and luxury.

- I enjoy providing beautiful service to others.

- I naturally feel drawn to giving and
sharing my gifts, time, and resources.

- I know that this is an infinite universe,
with plenty for everyone.

- When I observe the blessings and good
fortune of others, I feel happy.

- I love to pamper myself and give myself gifts.

- When I spend time and money on
treats for myself, I feel great.

- I allow myself breaks, treats, and vacations.

- I take time to enjoy the little things.

- Literally and figuratively, I stop
  and smell the flowers.

- I concentrate more on what I have
  and less on what I don't have.

- When I desire something, I look forward
  to receiving it with joyful anticipation.

- I enjoy my present blessings and excitedly
  look forward to the blessings in my future.

- I feel good about receiving wealth,
  because I know that the more I
  have, the more I have to give.

- I enjoy donating time, energy, and
  resources to causes I care about.

- I enjoy receiving gifts and all forms of support.

- I know that if I feel grateful for something
  before it appears in my present life experience,
  it is only a matter of time before it does appear.

- I always have more than enough.

- Money and resources seem to flow to
  me naturally and almost effortlessly.

Qualities Associated with the Prosperity Key

The following descriptions are designed to help you determine how well the prosperity key is already flowing in your
life, and also to begin creating subtle shifts that will prepare
you to more fully activate it.

WEALTH AND ABUNDANCE

Why do we want to be wealthy? So that we can have a bunch of fancy-looking paper and see a large number when we look at our bank balance? No! Paper and digital numbers have no real value in and of themselves. We want to be wealthy because we think that wealth will translate into happiness and other good feelings. In other words, when we say we want to be wealthy, what we really mean is that we want to feel things like comfort, safety, confidence, happiness, excitement, freedom, and joy. So when we focus on these feelings and find them in our lives right now, our prosperity key becomes activated; we are already wealthy. And it is a magical and metaphysical principle that *what we focus on expands*, so the wealthier we feel, the wealthier we become. Money and financial success are simply physical representations of this internal state, and when your prosperity key is activated in this way, they will unfailingly begin to appear in your life.

AFFLUENCE

Affluence is an aspect and extension of the above qualities of wealth and abundance. The word *affluence* contains a root word root that translates to "flow," and when we are affluent, we are a flowing fountain of wealth: it unendingly flows from us, to us, and through us.

GRATITUDE

Gratitude is the prosperity key's lifeblood. When we are grateful, we are concentrating on our blessings, and (as I alluded to above), when we concentrate on our blessings, no matter what our bank account looks like, we are already prosperous, and we're getting more so by the second. When we connect with the riches (in whatever form) that we already possess, our riches—on both internal and external planes of reality—can't help but expand. This is the true meaning of the phrase "the rich get richer."

What's more, gratitude is its own reward: when we feel grateful, we feel good and we feel blessed, so in that moment we are prosperous. And the more moments of gratitude we experience, the more prosperous we become.

LUXURY

Consider the luxurious splendor of an almond orchard in bloom, a field of multicolored tulips, a forest of fragrant pines, or the rolling blue ocean stretching out as far as the eye can see. The Divine is obviously a big proponent of luxury, and as a child of the Divine, you are meant to experience luxury as a matter of course. When you find yourself in the flow of luxury and allow yourself to receive it with gratitude and joy, you will perceive that the Divine, and the divine spark within you, is pleased.

Or, you might think of it this way: the God/dess lives within you. Your little temporary self is an illusion; your true self is one with the God/dess. Enjoying luxury is an offering to the Divine in you and a celebration of your present life as an altar in the temple of divinity.

Practice: LUXURY IS ALWAYS IN THE BUDGET

What luxurious treat can you gift yourself with today: a sea-salt bath? A rose-petal foot soak? A walk outside with a loved one? An old movie in your favorite satin pajamas? A slowly savored organic chocolate bar? A few drops of essential oil in a diffuser?

GENEROSITY

As we've seen, wealth is not about paper and numbers. It's about the qualities we really want when we say we want to be wealthy: happiness, freedom, comfort, etc. This is why someone can be rich beyond belief in the eyes of the world and still, deep down, be poverty-stricken, or why someone can have a very small bank balance and still feel blessed and wealthy beyond her fondest dreams. When we feel truly wealthy—when we feel all the qualities that we really crave when we say we want wealth—we feel happy to share because we know that our supply comes from an infinite source, and we know that when we send something out with generosity and good will, it will always come back to us multiplied.

My dad is a wonderful example of this principle in action. He is wealthy in all ways: in the eyes of the world and in his heart. He always has what he needs, and he is always happy to share with others. He tells me, "It's the darndest thing: whenever I give someone something, I always receive even more. Since I figured this out, I've had more money than I've ever had before. It really works. I don't know how, but it does." He has a fortune from a fortune cookie stuck on his refrigerator that says: "The more you give, the more you have."

This principle is true not just with money but also with time, energy, and resources.

Practice: GREASING THE GENEROSITY WHEELS

When we give, it's important that we do so with an open heart and that we fully release whatever we are giving. In other words, if we give and immediately wish we hadn't or wonder if it might not have been such a good idea, we are erasing the energetic effect of our efforts. However, the more goodwill and generosity we can conjure up when we donate, the more positive effects we will receive. So if you don't yet feel comfortable donating something, don't! Start with what you feel comfortable donating. For example, maybe you have some clothes in your closet that you'll never wear again. Pack them up and donate them. Or maybe you can put a few cans of food in a food drive. Even sending beautiful energy and prayers to a person, group, or the entire planet can yield very substantial returns. Whatever you can give, give—and begin to notice the blessings that you receive in return.

ALLOWING

Prosperity is our natural state. It flows through our lives like water flows through a rushing river or wind flows through the treetops. Experiencing prosperity is simply a matter of *allowing* it to take its natural course, allowing it to abundantly flow into our life experience.

But since allowing is more of a "not doing" than a "doing," it might be helpful to examine what we are doing that might be blocking our natural allowance. For example, if any of the following limiting beliefs seem to be true for you, they are currently blocking your allowing. Recognizing and then letting go of the belief will help clear your channel so that you can allow prosperity to resume its natural flow.

- I do not deserve wealth.

- Wealthy people are unhappy.

- Luxury is for other people, not me.

- This is a limited universe, so when I receive, others go without.

- Life is hard.

- Wealthy people are annoying.

- No one likes rich people.

- You've got to work hard and do things you don't like if you want to be prosperous.

- I don't have time to pamper myself.

- If I take time to pamper myself, it means I am a bad parent or spouse.

- If I spend money on myself, it means I am a bad parent or spouse.

- If I experience wealth and prosperity, I am betraying my parents or showing them up.

- It's stressful to have a lot of money.

- Money is evil.

Practice: CLEARING THE CHANNEL

Look into your river of prosperity and see what limiting beliefs might be blocking the flow. You might discover a limiting belief listed here, or you might find others. Once you do, make a list. Then find five examples of ways each belief isn't true or doesn't have to be true. Write those down, then safely burn the pages, flush the ashes down the toilet, and wash your hands. Next, to reinforce your newly cleared channel and reshape your internal landscape, choose a prosperity affirmation from the end of this chapter and write it twenty times. Then craft something beautiful (a collage, painting, mobile, or embroidered pillow) that contains the affirmation, and display it in the prosperity area of your home. (For added punch, incorporate colors and symbols from this chapter too.)

MANIFESTATION

A true desire is a part of you—an expression of your personal essence. You can tell something's a true desire when your heart energy moves upward like champagne bubbles when you imagine receiving it. No matter what the object of your true desire might be, if it's a true desire, it's never greedy or selfish or shallow. Whether it's a Lamborghini, a career in the Peace Corps, a pair of sparkly red high heels, or meeting the love of your life, moving toward it will bring you joy and add a beautiful brushstroke to the work of art that is your life.

Discerning your true desires, moving toward them with joyful anticipation, and finally welcoming them into your present life experience is the art of manifestation and an important aspect of the prosperity key.

Practice: TRUE OR FALSE?

An important aspect of manifestation is sorting out the true desires from the false ones. False desires are things that we think we should want rather than things we actually want. For example, my boyfriend and I have been happily together for over twelve years. So many people ask us why we aren't married that I sometimes begin to think that I should want to get married, even though, try as I might, it doesn't necessarily make my heart sing to consider it. I don't hate the idea by any means; I just don't particularly desire it. I feel like we're married already, and to me, planning a wedding seems like a great big chore. To others, getting married is one of the highlights of their lives, and perhaps to me it will be one day, but right now it's just not one of my true desires. Going to Hawaii together? Yes. Staying together forever? Yes. Planning a wedding? Not so much.

So make a list of all the things you think you want. Then take a moment with each. Close your eyes and take some deep breaths. Imagine receiving it, and believe that it is already in your experience. Does your heart sing? If it does, circle the desire. If it doesn't, consider why you may have thought that you desired that particular item. Perhaps your mom convinced you that you wanted it or it was a societal norm or maybe when you were in junior high you decided you wanted it and you never really questioned it once you grew up. Once you're sure it's a false desire, cross it out. Letting go of the false desires and concentrating on the true ones will align you with your true self and clear the way for true prosperity.

Practice: DAILY MANIFESTATION

At least once a day, perhaps as part of your daily meditation, first thing in the morning or just before bed, close your eyes and envision the things you'd like to bring into your present life experience. Feel as if they're already true, and feel intense gratitude for them. Finish by thinking about the present blessings in your life, and feel intense gratitude for them in a similar way.

As you practice this, you might find that your desires begin to change in large or small ways. For example, maybe when you began you wanted a red Prius and now a silver one seems way more fun, or perhaps first you wanted to move to a beach house and then you realized you really want to live in the forest. This is an important aspect of the art of manifestation, and it simply means that you're getting even more in alignment with your true self and your true desires.

ENJOYMENT

If we're going to live up to the enormous sacred gift that is this present life, we need to do things like take breaks, spend time with our loved ones, go on vacations, walk barefoot in the grass, dangle our feet in the pool, and eat at our favorite restaurants. We need to recognize that these things aren't diversions; they're the main event. If we win an Academy Award or Pulitzer Prize, that's great, but it won't even begin to make up for the crime of not taking time to enjoy our life.

When our prosperity key is activated and flowing, we do enjoy life, and we understand the value of soaking up the beauty and preciousness of our present life experience.

Prosperity Key-Related Situations

Life situations and intentions that are related to the prosperity key include:

- Manifesting your desires

- Enjoying life

- Spending quality time with loved ones

- Taking breaks and vacations

- Treating and pampering yourself

- Counting your blessings

- Manifesting wealth and financial success

- Experiencing luxury

- Receiving money

- Prospering on all levels

- Receiving blessings in all forms

- Feeling blessed and lucky

- Being in the flow of abundance

- Experiencing financial windfalls

- Enjoying what you have while happily anticipating what you desire

Prosperity Key Affirmations

I am blessed beyond my fondest dreams.

I happily receive large amounts of wealth and abundance.

I am in the flow of divine prosperity.

I dwell in luxury.

I am a money magnet.

I am a divine child, and I receive wealth and abundance
by divine right.

Luxury is my birthright.

Wealth is my birthright.

I prosper on all levels.

I allow my wealth to flow.

I happily receive abundance.

I am divine prosperity.

Affluence is my true nature.

I am a fountain of prosperity.

The Alchemy of Prosperity

You might think of the prosperity key as a golden fountain of
light that endlessly flows through you and to you. When you
are in touch with this flow—when you consistently trust it,
expect it, and feel gratitude for it—it manifests in visible form
as money, resources, and all forms of blessings. The information in this chapter can help you work with both seen and
unseen worlds *and* in the place between the worlds so that
you can align with this infinite, divine flow of wealth and
experience the luxury and blessings that are your birthright.

Prosperity Key Symbols

THE NUMBER FOUR

In countless cultures, four is considered to be the number of the earth and the entire visible world. There are four seasons in a year, four corners in a room, and four building blocks to all physical matter in both ancient cosmologies (earth, air, water, and fire) and modern ones (protons, neutrons, electrons, and electron neutrinos).

Here are some ideas for activating the prosperity key with the number four:

- Place four chrysocolla crystals (see page 228) in the prosperity area of your home. Choose an affirmation from earlier in the chapter. Direct your palms and the energy of your words toward the crystals as you repeat the affirmation sixteen times (count four times four).

- Place four small jade plants or four vases of living bamboo in the prosperity area and similarly empower them.

- Create a necklace or bracelet with four jade beads. On a Thursday during a waxing moon, empower them with your intention to activate the prosperity key, then wear them.

AN AFFLUENT VIBE AND THINGS THAT
SEEM (OR ARE) EXPENSIVE

One of the main principles of alchemy and magic of all kinds is that when you clearly, consistently, and potently experience the feeling related to a certain blessing or situation before it appears in the physical realm, it is only a matter of time before it appears.

With this in mind, when your home and the items you're surrounded with on a daily basis give you the feeling of prosperity, you are harmonizing yourself with the energy of the prosperity key. As such, you will begin to receive more prosperity in the physical realm (or to appreciate the prosperity you already have in a more nourishing way), which in turn will help you become even more aligned with the prosperity key. Entering into this ever-expanding cycle is known as getting in the flow of prosperity, and it's another demonstration of the principle behind the saying "the rich get richer."

Here are some ideas for activating the prosperity key with them:

- Look around your home and make small, free, or inexpensive changes that create a more affluent feeling: clean or paint the front door, replace burned-out light bulbs, light shadowed areas in your yard or home, get a new doormat, replace tattered curtains, get a bath mat that makes you feel like you're at a spa.

- Find a purse or wallet that makes you feel
  wealthy (it doesn't matter if these items are
  actually expensive or just seem expensive).

- Take stock of your wardrobe and decide
  if there are a few inexpensive items you
  could add that would make you feel more
  luxurious when you're getting dressed: an
  ample supply of socks, underwear you love,
  a belt that matches your favorite shoes, etc.

- When shopping for clothes and décor,
  whenever possible choose items that give
  you the feeling of wealth and prosperity.

- If you have a favorite décor item or furniture
  piece that makes you feel wealthy every
  time you look at it, consider placing it
  in the prosperity area of your home (if
  it fits and feels right there, of course).

- When possible and appropriate, choose sensual
  textures and sumptuous materials for your
  home, especially in the prosperity area.

REPRESENTATIONS OR SYMBOLS
OF WEALTH AND ABUNDANCE

There are a lot of images and symbols that can represent
wealth; for example, an orchard in fruit, a horn of plenty, a
charm of Chinese coins woven together with red string, a
gorgeous ship sailing in to shore. In short, if a painting, sculpture, charm, print, or other symbolic item speaks to your

sense of prosperity and abundance, it can help activate the prosperity key in your life.

Here are some ideas for activating the prosperity key with them:

- Choose images related to wealth and abundance when decorating the prosperity area of your home.

- Place a feng shui charm made from Chinese coins in the prosperity area of your home. Direct your palms toward it, close your eyes, conjure up the feeling of experiencing immense prosperity, and repeat an affirmation from earlier in this chapter sixteen times (count four times four).

- On a Wednesday night during a waxing moon, place a real gold coin or a silver dollar coin in a small dish of sea salt. Leave it in the salt overnight. The next day, remove it and hold it between your two palms. Hold your hands at your heart in prayer pose. Conjure up feelings related to comfort, wealth, and prosperity. Repeat an affirmation from earlier in this chapter nine times. Place the coin between your mattress and box spring so that it's directly beneath you as you sleep. (Flush the salt down the toilet or pour it down the drain—do not eat it!)

FLOWING WATER

Where clear water flows, people and plants prosper. What's more, flowing water generates negative ions, which is the scientific term for good vibes. As if that weren't enough, abundantly and constantly flowing water is a powerful visual affirmation of abundantly and constantly flowing wealth. This shows up in our language in terms like affluence (with the word root that means "flow"), cash flow, and liquid assets.

Here are some ideas for activating the prosperity key with it:

- Place a fountain in the prosperity area of your home. (Provided it is not the bedroom* and it fits attractively.)

- Choose flowing water imagery (fountains, waterfalls, seascapes) for the prosperity area of your home.*

- Because water represents and holds the energy of wealth and prosperity, managing and regulating your home's water flow is also important. In essence, this means fixing leaks immediately, adding nozzles where necessary to slow unpleasantly excessive water flow, and keeping your toilet lid closed to prevent energy and attention from being drawn into the toilet bowl and to contain energy within the room. (Please don't obsess if you have especially recalcitrant roommates or family members—harmony is more important than a consistently closed toilet seat.)

- Get a reusable water bottle that you love. Using a marker or tape, write or attach the word *prosperity* to the outside of the bottle to infuse your water with the energy of this life key. Drink at least half your body weight in ounces per day. (Additionally or instead, you might write or attach the word to your water pitcher.)

* **Because we want to create a grounded and solid feeling in the bedroom, fountains and watery design pieces in this area are generally not ideal.**

HEALTHY PLANTS

Where plants thrive, humans thrive. And when we are surrounded with healthy plants, we feel relaxed, nourished, and safe. Needless to say, these feelings are in alignment with, and powerfully activate, the prosperity key.

All plants with a lush and vibrant feeling activate the prosperity key, but houseplants that are especially in alignment with this key include pothos, jade, corn plant, bamboo, and Norfolk Island pine. (Generally speaking, sharp, bladelike plants and prickly cacti will not do the trick.)

Here are some ideas for activating the prosperity key with them:

- Keep healthy plants in and around your home or workplace.

- Place healthy plants in the prosperity area of your home.

- Spend time in lush green landscapes and soak in the prosperity key energy.

- Choose imagery depicting healthy plants and lush nature scenery for the prosperity area of your home.

Prosperity Key Deities

Divinities that are associated with wealth, luck, and abundance are especially in alignment with the prosperity key. Below you'll find some that fall into these categories. To help activate and heal your relationship with this key, you might strike up a relationship with any or all of them. You might also wear jewelry depicting one of them or display one or more of them in the prosperity area of your home or on your altar.

LAKSHMI

The beautiful Hindu goddess of wealth and luxury, Lakshmi is often depicted near a flowing river or fountain, surrounded by an abundance of sparkling golden coins. She reminds us that wealth is our birthright, aligns us with the energy of luxury, and enhances the relaxed positivity that comes from knowing that, now and always, we have everything we need. She sometimes appears with Ganesh, the elephant-headed deity who removes obstacles and provides swift assistance.

LAUGHING BUDDHA (HOTEI, MAITREYA)

Hotei may appear as a fat, bald man with missing teeth, but that doesn't stop him from laughing with joy over his endless good fortune. Golden statues of the laughing Buddha are traditionally placed in the home to increase wealth and all forms of blessings. Simply gazing at an image of him (or rubbing his head) can lift your spirits and activate your prosperity key in a powerful way.

ABUNDANTIA

Abundantia, the cornucopia-carrying goddess of ancient Rome, is the personification of the energy associated with the prosperity key. If we call on her, she protects and increases our financial flow, and it's said while we sleep she'll visit our homes bearing gifts of abundant prosperity.

THREE LUCKY GODS

To activate the prosperity key, traditional feng shui practitioners often recommend placing statues of the three lucky gods—Fuk (the god of blessings), Luk (the god of wealth), and Sau (the god of vibrant health and well being)—in the home.

Prosperity Key Animals

Like deities, each animal carries its own unique qualities and helpful energy. To activate the prosperity key in your life, you can work with the animals below through meditation, prayer, altars, or imagery in your home, on your altar, or on your person (as in jewelry or tattoos).

MANEKI NEKO (AND ALL CATS)

Cats of all kinds are said to summon luck and are excellent examples of dwelling in relaxation and feeling entitled to all of the luxuries that life has to offer. Maneki Neko is not just any cat. She's the cat you often see waving to you in your local Chinatown and near the entrance to Asian restaurants. She appears in many colors, and each color represents a specific type of blessing that she welcomes into the home or business where she resides. For basic prosperity key purposes, choose a statue or picture with her right hand raised. You might place her near your entrance, on your altar, or in the prosperity area of your home. Here's a basic key to her colors and the types of blessings that each one summons:

> **White:** Happiness, purity, luck
>
> **Gold:** Financial wealth
>
> **Yellow:** Happy home, marital bliss
>
> **Red:** Health, protection, passion, love
>
> **Pink:** Romance, keeping children happy and safe
>
> **Green:** Health, higher education
>
> **Purple:** Creativity, harmonious dreams

KOI AND GOLDFISH

Koi and goldfish represent the vibrant, swirling, flowing nature of abundant blessings and wealth.

FROG

Frogs summon and symbolize luck, abundance, affluence, and wishes that come true.

Prosperity Key Colors

To activate or enhance the prosperity key in your life, you might work with any or all of the following colors, perhaps in one or more of the following ways:

- Wear one or more of them.

- Obtain one candle in one of the colors. Charge it with a prosperity-related intention, place it in your prosperity area, and light it. Extinguish when necessary and light again when possible until it burns all the way down.

- Decorate with one or more of the colors in any combination in the prosperity area of your home.

    Red: A color of wealth, confidence, personal power, luck, and success, red is naturally aligned with the prosperity key in a powerful way.

    Purple: "Even redder than red" (according to old feng shui wisdom), a touch of the fluid color blue takes the wealth-related blessings of red even further by enhancing its depth and luxury to create purple.

Blue: With the fluidity of water and the vibrant, growing movement associated with the wood element, blue unites the energies of cool nourishment and upward expansion.

Green: The color of money and of lush, livable landscapes.

Metallic Gold: Touches of this luxurious, sparkly sheen give us the feeling of sumptuous wealth and nourishing, expansive, all-encompassing sunshine.

Prosperity Key Herbs

CLOVE

The energy of cloves is sweet, comforting, and expansive, and it infuses our consciousness with the essence of wealth. Try:

- Diffusing clove essential oil.

- Making a prosperity potion with hot apple cider, cinnamon, and a hint of cloves.

- Decorating an orange by piercing it with whole cloves. Tie it up with green and gold ribbons and hang it near the entrance or in a window in the prosperity

area of your home to bless your life with
wealth and activate the prosperity key.

PATCHOULI

Provided we enjoy the scent, nothing brings us to our
senses and wraps us in a feeling of ultimate wellbeing exactly
like patchouli.

Try:

- Diffusing essential oil of patchouli.

- Wearing patchouli as a perfume (or adding
  it to your lotion or favorite scent).

- Anointing your wealth charms with a few
  drops of patchouli oil before empowering
  them or to refresh their magical potency.

SAFFRON

It takes a lot of saffron flowers to produce one tiny bottle
of the little saffron stigmas that we use to season our food,
which is why it's widely believed to be the most expensive of
all kitchen spices. This fact, along with the fact that its scent,
color, and taste all exude differing manifestations of prosperity key energy, make it a powerful wealth-drawing herb.

Try:

- Placing a pinch of saffron in a red flannel bag
  along with four silver dollars and a citrine
  quartz. Tie it closed with a golden ribbon and
  hang it in the prosperity area of your home.

- Performing a little kitchen witchery by adding saffron to your meal and chanting a prosperity affirmation over it sixteen times while it's cooking or being prepared.

Prosperity Key Crystals

To receive the prosperity key–enhancing benefits of any of the crystals below, wear or carry one of them or place one of them in the prosperity area of your home. You may also empower one or both them with any of the prosperity key affirmations that appear earlier in this chapter.

CHRYSOCOLLA

This playful, vibrant, delightful teal crystal helps open your floodgates to abundance by reminding you that prosperity is your natural state.

CITRINE QUARTZ

Considered the wealth-drawing crystal by many magical and metaphysical practitioners, citrine helps activate the prosperity key by reminding us of the happy, light-hearted, eternally flowing fountain of wellbeing that we are in truth.

JADE

Jade is a traditional luck- and prosperity-drawing crystal that sensualizes us, soothes us, and brings us into harmony with the easy, breezy, heart-pleasing luxury that is only awaiting our recognition.

Prosperity Key Master Ritual

If, after reading through this entire book once, you determine that the prosperity key is the key that could use the most help in your life right now, performing the following ritual will activate and calibrate this key for you in an ideal way. Or perform this ritual anytime that you feel that your prosperity key is in need of some major help.

Because the art of bliss is a holistic science, not only will your prosperity key benefit from this ritual, but every other life key will benefit as well.

Please note: the synchronicity key nourishes the prosperity key in a powerful way, so if you feel that your synchronicity key could use some help as well, you may want to start there and move on to this key later. Once you've considered the provided information, the bottom line when deciding where to start, of course, is to tune in to your intuition and follow it.

INGREDIENTS

A compass

4 green votive or small jar candles

A stick or cone of patchouli incense and a holder

A tall red jar candle or red three-wick candle

A wineglass or chalice of pure water

A small or medium-sized potted jade plant

A lighter or matches

On a Thursday when the moon is new, waxing, or full, shower or bathe. Dress in something clean that feels both comfortable and elegant (any sort of day, night, or ritual wear that feels right will do). Position the green candles on the floor so that they will be surrounding you during the ritual. Use the compass to place them at the four compass points of an invisible circle that is roughly six feet in diameter. Near the eastern candle, place the incense and holder. Near the southern candle, place the red candle. Near the western candle, place the chalice of water. Near the northern candle, place the potted jade.

Stand in the center of the circle, facing east. Rest comfortably in your body. Close your eyes and take some deep breaths. Visualize a vacuum tube of light vacuuming your entire body and aura and the space within the circle. See this vacuum removing any and all negativity from these areas. Now light the candle in front of you (the one at the east of the circle). Move in a clockwise direction as you light the southern, western, and northern candles respectively. See yourself surrounded in a circle of golden-white flame, connecting and encompassing the candles. Now stand facing east once more. Say:

**I now summon the winds of fortune and
the guardians of the four directions.**

Light the incense. While still facing east, with your hands relaxed and down by your sides, face your palms outward toward the east in a receptive posture. Say:

**Guardians of the east, I call you and
welcome you into the circle. East wind**

> of fortune—airy wind of freshness,
> movement, and new ideas—I summon
> you now and welcome you into my life.

Close your eyes and visualize/imagine/feel the fortunate blessings of the east wind caressing you and flowing generously into your life.

Turn toward the south. Light the red candle. Stand in the receptive posture again. Say:

> Guardians of the south, I call on you and
> welcome you into the circle. South
> wind of fortune—fiery wind of passion,
> courage, and raging success—I summon
> you now and welcome you into my life.

Close your eyes and feel the south wind warming you, enlivening you, and setting your life on fire with blessings.

Turn toward the west. Place your hands on either side of the chalice or glass, then dip your hand in the water and anoint your brow, throat, heart, and belly. Stand in the receptive posture once more. Say:

> Guardians of the west, I call on you and
> welcome you into the circle. West wind
> of fortune—watery wind of affluence,
> authenticity, and divine flow—I summon
> you now and welcome you into my life.

Close your eyes and feel this cool wind enhancing your spirit and infusing your life with an unlimited flow of wealth and prosperity.

Turn toward the north. Place your hands on either side of the potted jade. Harmonize with its earthy, grounded nature, and feel your connection to the earth. Stand in the receptive posture. Say:

> Guardians of the north, I call on you and
>   welcome you into the circle. North wind of
>   fortune—earthy wind of security, comfort,
>   and generous abundance—I summon you
>   now and welcome you into my life.

Close your eyes and feel this sensual wind grounding you in the physical realm and gifting your life with unlimited sustenance and every luxury you could possibly desire.

Slowly spin in a clockwise direction with your arms outstretched, luxuriating in the now generously flowing four winds of fortune. Face north once more. Say:

> For as long as I have existed, blessings
>   of all forms have been seeking
>   me from all directions.
> Today is the day that I allow
>   myself to receive them.
> Winds of fortune, welcome.
> Here I am.
> Thank you for being here.
> Thank you for providing everything
>   that I want and need, and more.

I now receive your gifts with joy and
with a degree of gratitude that
exceeds all comprehension.
I promise to share with an open heart
and to keep the prosperity flowing.
Thank you, thank you, thank you.

Now, while still facing north, say:

Guardians of the north, thank you.

Turn to the west and say:

Guardians of the west, thank you.

Turn toward the south and say:

Guardians of the south, thank you.

Turn toward the east and say:

Guardians of the east, thank you.

Now extinguish all the candles in a counterclockwise order. Finish by lying flat on the ground and relaxing for at least five minutes to ground yourself. Then eat something earthy like a baked potato, flax crackers and hummus, or some toast.

8 | Resilience

All around you and into the far distance in every direction is a forest. Beneath your feet roots grow deep. Above your head a canopy of green stretches across the sky. Through the leaves you can see dark rainclouds that cast a shadow over the landscape. Thunder rolls. Raindrops begin to lightly fall, and a cold wind blows. You pull your coat more tightly around yourself and feel certain that a storm is close at hand. Because you feel connected to the plants, the animals, the sky above, and the earth beneath your feet, you feel ancient, eternal, and ready for anything. You know that before you, after you, in the present moment, and beyond the illusion of time, eternity dwells. Life is nothing to fear because death will certainly arrive and wash all problems away, and death is nothing to fear because it is only a transition into another way of being. From this fearless, eternal perspective, your health thrives and your relationships heal.

**This is the alchemical essence of
life key #8: resilience.**

If the energies associated with this life key are flowing harmoniously, the following statements will be true for you (and
the more ideal the flow, the truer they will be):

- I know that challenges are a natural part of life,
  and I embrace them rather than fear them.

- When tragedy strikes, I am reminded of the
  profound beauty of life and of my deep love
  and appreciation for the people in my life.

- I know that no family is perfect, and
  I choose to embrace the process of
  forgiveness and healing surrounding
  my childhood and family issues.

- I know that I'm a part of something
  much bigger than my little human self.

- I feel connected to my ancestors or spiritual
  heritage and know that the origins of my
  present existence stretch further into the
  past than I can possibly comprehend.

- I honor my ancestors, past lives,
  and spiritual heritage.

- I see the earth as a living, breathing organism,
  and, like a DNA sample, I see myself as both
  a tiny part of that organism and as containing
  the entirety of that organism within my being.

- I embrace the continual process of releasing
  old karma and clearing old patterns.

- I feel eternal.

- I feel vast.

- I feel ready for anything.

- My family relationships and family issues seem to be getting better and better.

- I am vibrant, and my health seems to continually improve.

- When I encounter health issues, I examine them from all angles and work to heal them from a holistic perspective.

- When old family or childhood issues arise, I examine them from all angles and work to heal them from a holistic perspective.

- I realize that physical health issues, mental health issues, or childhood and family issues are not things to be feared but opportunities to heal and become stronger on all levels.

- Although I have a natural instinct for survival, and although I deeply enjoy the process of life, I do not fear death.

- I feel supported by my life conditions and by the people in my life.

Qualities Associated with the Resilience Key

The following descriptions are designed to help you determine how well the resilience key is already flowing in your life and also begin creating subtle shifts that will prepare you to more fully activate it.

VIBRANT HEALTH

In the 1960s, a team of researchers studied the small Italian settlement of Roseto, Pennsylvania, to attempt to discover how almost all its residents lived such exceptionally long, disease-free lives. After looking at all the usual suspects (diet, genetics, activity level, location), they finally determined that it was, in fact, the tightly knit families, vibrantly active social groups, and general connection and familiarity that supported the seemingly miraculous level of physical health of the community at large. This phenomenon is now often cited in scientific discussions about longevity and is known as "the Roseto Effect."

Similarly, when our resilience key is activated and flowing, we know that we are but one small part of a greater whole—a greater whole that includes not just our families but also all humans from all time periods (in the past, present, and future), plants, animals, and the entire planet. We feel relaxed, happy, and free of stress. As a result, we experience vibrant physical and mental health.

HARDINESS

Nietzsche wrote that "whatever doesn't kill me makes me stronger." And while this might not be precisely true in all cases, when it comes to childhood/family issues and emotional challenges, similar statements like "whatever doesn't kill you has the potential to make you stronger" or "whatever doesn't kill you is an opportunity to become stronger" might be more consistently accurate. Interestingly, these statements might also be true in a number of cases related to health, exercise, and immunity.

My favorite thing about this perspective is that it allows us to get out of victim consciousness. Instead of "poor me, look what happened to me," we get to say this: "That experience was difficult, to say the least, but I wouldn't trade it for anything, because it infused me with wisdom and healing abilities that I otherwise would not have had." We get to say, "Oh yeah? You think you're going to negatively affect my life in a long-term way? Well, guess what: no dice. And guess what else: I'm going to end up even stronger and wiser than before." Sure, some shadows may be cast for a while, but with the resilience that is built into the human spirit, we have the potential to eventually move out of them and into the light. And besides, without a few shadows, the constant brightness would get boring, and the lack of contrast would wash out all the beauty.

Even when you're in the middle of a particularly bitter challenge, this perspective can lift your spirits and help you to see the bigger picture. As a matter of fact, it got me through many a challenging moment in my childhood and adolescence. I remember thinking: "In a way this is great, because it will build character. One day I am going to have *so much character*!" (And I think it's worth noting that I was right!)

Similarly, when I have a cold, I think, "This is excellent. Now my immune system can get some exercise, and I won't be due for another cold for a good long while."

Like a healthy tree with deep roots, when our resilience key is activated and flowing, we can bend with the wind and remain standing after the storm has passed.

We know that toughing it out and pushing ourselves to new heights can bring benefits in a number of life areas, including exercise, competitive endeavors, healing illnesses, breaking old habits, and manifesting our dreams. We might even begin to welcome challenges rather than shrink from them, because we understand the wealth of potential benefits each challenge contains.

WILLINGNESS TO FORGIVE

When we hang on to our pain and refuse to be willing to forgive, it doesn't do us any good and it doesn't do the object of our grudges any harm either. In fact, it's quite the opposite. We stay miserable and our former tormentor remains a powerful figure in our lives. Energetically, even if we haven't seen this person (or group) for years, or even if this person is dead or this group has been disbanded, we remain tied to him/her/them as we continue to give away our power by saying, "You did this to me, and just look at the power you still have to keep me down and cause me harm."

When we realize the truth of this, we are naturally willing to forgive because we don't want to stay in this power-draining relationship any longer. We want to reclaim our power by remembering that *we* are the deciding factor when it comes to our own happiness; no one else has the ability to diminish our enjoyment of life. Being willing to forgive is the only requirement. Once we are authentically willing, and we state this willingness to the universe and to ourselves, it is only a matter of time before our intuition and destiny lead us down the path of forgiveness so we can heal. Then, our past garbage becomes compost for the fragrant garden that is our present moment and beautiful future.

Practice: FORGIVENESS INVENTORY

What grudges, grievances, and old hurts are you still hanging on to? Where in your life have you not forgiven? Make a list of who you haven't forgiven and what you haven't forgiven them for (include yourself, if applicable). Keep writing for at least fifteen minutes or for a full two pages' worth to make sure that you dredge up everything you possibly can at this time. When this feels complete, for each one say or write: *I am willing to forgive* _____ *for* _____. Say it more than once if it doesn't ring true the first time, and remind yourself that you want to forgive *for your own benefit* and not for the sake of anyone else.

HEALING CHILDHOOD ISSUES

When we adopt the "whatever doesn't kill me makes me stronger" perspective and when we choose to forgive for the sake of our own well-being, healing childhood issues becomes a beloved hobby rather than a source of uneasiness and dread. Every time we uncover an issue and free ourselves from its thrall, we are that much lighter, more successful, and more joyful. It's not that it isn't painful to work through old issues, it's just that we realize that the pain is going to be there anyway, whether we consciously feel it or not. And when we do consciously feel it, we begin to shift it, transmute it, and move through it so that we can free up the stagnant energy it once contained. In effect, we're retrieving a formerly locked-up piece of our spirit so that we can be more spiritually complete and have all of our energetic cylinders firing.

HEALING PAST–LIFE ISSUES

Sometimes recurring challenges in our present life stem from challenges in our past lives. Whether we consciously remember these challenges or not, just as with our childhood issues, we have the opportunity to heal from them and liberate the trapped energy they contain. When our resilience key is activated and flowing, we enter into this healing process as a matter of course.

HEALING OLD FAMILY PATTERNS

Similarly, certain challenges can sometimes be built into a family dynamic (such as certain kinds of abuse or mental illness), and these challenges can go on for generations. When we have a healthy relationship with our resilience key, we can break these family curses once and for all, thereby allowing all future generations to be free of them. We can say that "the buck stops here."

Practice: WHAT BUCKS STOP WITH YOU?

On both sides of my family, I can see a history of powerful females who have dimmed or hidden their light, bringing about dire consequences in the areas of mental health and family harmony. I chose to let that buck stop with me. By allowing my power to shine, I intend to not only heal future generations, but to send healing and release to the past generations as well.

What bucks stop with you? Make a list. Then brainstorm steps you can take toward doing the inner work necessary to exorcise this issue from your consciousness, and consequently from your family tree.

LETTING GO OF GUILT AND BLAME

When our emotions are clean and pure, no matter what emotions they are (even if we're sobbing or our heart is aching), they feel deeply satisfying on a certain level because they allow our spirits to flow and they remind us that we are alive and that life is beautiful. Guilt and blame are not actual emotions, and they make it difficult for us to feel grief, rage, and other "negative" emotions in a clean and healthy way. In fact, we might call them "false emotions" because they stem from premises that are untrue. For example, guilt and blame would not be possible without the following beliefs:

- Things happen that "shouldn't" have happened. (If something happened, we know that it, in fact, *should* have happened, because it *did* happen. When we pretend we can see the big picture and know what should and shouldn't have happened, we enter into a battle with what is, and that battle is a waste of time and energy because we will always lose it. It is a much better use of energy to work with what is rather than to give energy to what we think "should have been.")

- Other people have power over us to keep us down and cause us harm. (Only our own reactions have the power to do these things.)

- It's our responsibility to make others happy. (Everyone is responsible for his or her own happiness.)

- Others have the responsibility to make us happy. (We are responsible for our own happiness.)

- We have the power to make other people sad. (Only their reactions have that power.)

- Other people have the power to make us sad. (Only our reactions have that power.)

- People don't always do the very best they can with what they know and where they are emotionally at any given time. (We all want to do what's best. Deep down, we all want to dwell in love and act out of love, but when we don't, it's because we are ill in some way or we don't have the tools or the understanding we need at that particular moment.)

Needless to say, at certain times we will still very likely discover that we are harboring guilt or blame. But when our resilience key is activated and flowing, we choose to proactively release them so that our emotions can flow in a healing, nourishing, and nontoxic way.

FEELING CONNECTED TO ANCESTORS AND HERITAGE

My mom loves plants, and I do too. Since I was a child, she's pointed to wildflowers and herbs and told me their names and what they're used for. My Irish-American grandfather, Papa Harry (my mom's dad), was a landscaper and a farmer. He taught my mom the names of plants when she was a child, and now I have his old wildflower and herb books on my shelf. I feel in my blood that this herbal fascination goes back for countless generations and connects me to Ireland and the Old Ways.

Feelings like this give us a sense of continuity. They enhance our present by grounding us in the past. They remind us that we are not alone in time: we are a leaf on an ancient tree whose existence extends for centuries into the past and future.

Even if we're adopted or don't know a lot about our ancestors or heritage, we can consciously connect with our blood and listen to our inner knowing about who we are and where we come from.

HEALTHY (OR HEALING) FAMILY RELATIONSHIPS

For two years during my early twenties, I didn't speak to my mom at all. When I was in high school, I refused to visit my dad for my entire junior and senior years. Now (thanks to the benefits of an activated resilience key)—after a number of meditations, visualizations, journal entries, arguments, and heart-to-heart talks—I can honestly say that I love hanging out with both of them.

Even for those family members with whom we feel an active relationship may not be desirable or possible, we can still connect with the true, healed, divine part of them on the energetic level. We can also release guilt and blame and thereby detoxify our emotions toward them, and we can work to forgive them: not for their sake, but for the sake of our own personal empowerment and healing.

FEELING CONNECTED TO EVERYTHING

Perhaps the most basic, essential benefit of an activated resilience key is feeling connected to everything and feeling that everything is connected. We are not just in a family relationship with our parents, children, aunts, uncles, grandparents, and cousins but also with the entire human race, all animals, all plants, the sun, the moon, the air, the water, and the earth beneath our feet. When we feel this connection, we feel vast and eternal; we feel that our life is meaningful and valuable, and we feel inspired by what the Buddhists would call the "suchness" of everything.

GOOD SOCIAL SUPPORT SYSTEM

My best friend Sedona lives in Portland, where there are a lot of trees and a lot of rain, both of which represent and emanate resilience key energy. Whenever I visit her, I envy the strong community spirit I feel everywhere we go: the cooperative health food stores, the well-attended local art events, the strong friendships, and the way so many people seem to be genuinely interested in the well-being of other people and the planet.

This might be the main reason so many people love Portland. After all, a large number of psychologists look to the social support system of their clients as a big factor in their happiness and emotional health.

Even if we don't live in an area that has the alchemy of the resilience key built in so powerfully (like Los Angeles, where I live), we can employ the information in this chapter to help manifest and reinforce a good social support system.

A HEALTHY RELATIONSHIP WITH DEATH

My family has been in the funeral business for at least three generations. When I was two or three, I remember looking up at the bottom side of a raised casket. All I knew was that it looked like a really fun box to play in, and I told my dad to put me in there. He smiled compassionately down at me and said, "You *really* want me to put you in there?" He lifted me up and let me gaze at a waxy woman with grey hair and a pink dress, positioned peacefully. At that moment, I understood that she was dead; I didn't think that she was sleeping. No one had to have "the talk" with me. I just knew, and while it was a surprise that there was a woman's body in the box I had wanted to play in, it wasn't a surprise that death existed. It was as if I had known it since the moment I was born, and I believe I had.

This powerful memory—along with the denial or unnatural terror I notice that death often seems to inspire in other people—leads me to believe that our culture's habit of shielding our children (and ourselves) from death does more harm than good, especially because death is such a necessary source of inspiration. For example, consider:

- Death lends poignancy to life. The fully embraced knowledge that we and all our loved ones will eventually transition out of this present form allows us to love bravely, live courageously, feel truly free, and surrender completely to the moment. (If you've ever lost someone dear to you, you know how powerfully it opens your heart to the beauty and divinity of that loved one and reminds you to appreciate your present moments and all those loved ones who are still here in their physical forms.)

- Death inspires a feeling of connection. Our physical existence is characterized by change. When we consider that nothing truly dies but only changes its appearance, we are reminded that we are, in fact, eternal, and that our energy is but one part of the greater whole.

- Death creates the space for life. If everything that was ever born retained its original physical form, we would have no room for new energy and new life. And because we know that nothing really dies but only changes, and that when things stay in one energetic form for too long they become stagnant and brittle, we know that this cycle of ending and beginning is what makes this kaleidoscopic existence so magical and marvelous.

• Death is the ultimate adventure. I love a good mystery, and what's more mysterious than the land beyond? And although I don't race toward death (it'll arrive soon enough, and I've got plenty to do in the meantime), I'm comforted by the idea that, as a grand finale to this present life experience, I will get to take an unknowable journey to the other side.

Resilience Key-Related Situations

Life situations and intentions that are related to the resilience key include:

• Healing childhood issues

• Healing past-life issues

• Healing systemic family issues

• Strengthening physical health

• Strengthening mental health

• Forgiving yourself and others

• Learning about your ancestors

• Discovering past lives

• Family gatherings

• Family-like gatherings

- Making long-term, family-like friendships
- Healing the family dynamic
- Communicating with family and family-like friends
- Moving through serious challenges
- Helping loved ones transition out of this life
- Making peace with death
- Strengthening your social support system
- Being a part of other people's social support system

Resilience Key Affirmations

I am willing to forgive.

I forgive everyone, and everyone forgives me.

I am one with everything.

I am supported and loved beyond measure.

I give and receive love and support.

My challenges are springboards to greater and greater levels of freedom.

Everything is a learning experience and an opportunity to heal.

I face my challenges with excitement and joy.

I transmute challenges into opportunities and blessings.

I embrace the process of life.

I embrace the mystery.

I am vast and eternal.

I am healthy, healed, and strong.

I am balanced, nourished, and vibrantly healthy.

My roots go deep, and my branches stretch wide.

I am nourished by life.

I allow myself to receive nourishment and support.

Ancient wisdom dwells within me.

I feel my feelings and allow myself to heal.

The Alchemy of Resilience

The resilience key roots you into the earth as it flows upward through your life experience, fortifying your spirit and emotions so that, like a healthy tree, you can stay firm, upright, and supple, and draw nourishment from even the heaviest of storms.

Resilience Key Symbols

THE NUMBER THREE

Miranda Lundy, author of *Sacred Number*, writes: "Three, like a tree, bridges heaven and earth. The triad…is the synthesis or return to unity after the division of two." Indeed, our individual self stands between earth and sky, and past and

251

future. When we are nourished by each polarity and realize that we contain each polarity, we feel complete, vast, and connected to everything.

Similarly, three sticks are harder to break than one or two; three strands woven together create a sturdy braid; a stool with three legs will never wobble; and we can even stand firm when we are upside down provided we connect solidly to the ground with three appendages (two hands and a head), all of which brings to mind Ecclesiastes 4:12: "Though one may be overpowered, two can defend themselves. A cord of three strands is not quickly broken."

Here are some ideas for activating the resilience key with the number three:

- Place three healthy plants side by side in the resilience area of your home.

- Safely stand on your head, or in a tripod position, for three minutes (work up to it).

- Braid together one strand each of green, teal, and blue cotton yarn as you repeat an affirmation from earlier in this chapter. Tie it around your wrist as a bracelet and resilience key charm or place in the resilience area of your home.

HEALTHY PLANTS

Healthy plants are powerful affirmations of health and resilience, and they remind us that we, like them, are living bridges between heaven and earth. By connecting with the soil, which is made up of composted and formerly decayed living matter, they also remind us that past, future, life, and death are connected in an endless dance. As if that weren't enough, they literally nourish our physical health by cleaning the air and infusing it with greater levels of oxygen.

Here are some ideas for activating the resilience key with them:

- Place healthy plants in the resilience area of your home.
- Place healthy plants near your entrance and in other areas of your home.
- Tend your garden.
- Spend time in nature.

TREES AND FORESTS

As you may have gathered, trees and forests might just be the most quintessential symbol of the resilience key. They connect earth and sky, remind us of resilience itself, connect us to the past and future, and demonstrate the interconnectedness of every single thing.

Here are some ideas for activating the resilience key with them:

- Choose imagery depicting trees and forests for the resilience area of your home.
- Take a walk in the forest.
- Go camping or vacationing in a forest.
- Spend time in quiet contemplation with a tree.

- Meditate with your spine against a tree.

- Hug a tree.

- Plant trees around your home.

- Cultivate a relationship with the trees around your home.

RAIN AND STORMS

Rain and storms, especially when coupled with trees and forests, are also quintessential symbols of this key. They remind us of the sayings "into every life a little rain must fall" and "April showers bring May flowers." Indeed, without precipitation, there would be no water to nourish the soil and feed the plants and wildlife. Not to mention, when we embrace them, much coziness and adventure can be derived from rainy, stormy days. Similarly, without challenges and shocks that upset the status quo, our lives would dry up. We'd not only begin to lack wisdom, sparkle, and dimension, we'd be insufferably bored (and boring).

Here are some ideas for activating the resilience key with them:

- Choose imagery depicting rain and storms for the resilience area of your home.

- Meditate on the resilience key during a rainstorm.

- Place a water fountain (small or large) in the resilience area of your home to invoke the nourishing power of rain.

- Place waterfall imagery in the resilience area of your home to depict emotional flow and invoke the downward movement of rain or a thunderstorm.

- Place a mirror in this area to invoke the energy of water.

THINGS MADE OF WOOD

Wood is nothing if not resilient. Additionally, it's made from trees, which are the most potent symbol of this key. Like it did while it was still growing, wood has a vibrant, supple, and upward energetic flow.

Here are some ideas for activating the resilience key with them:

- When possible and appropriate, choose wood furniture and décor pieces for the resilience area of your home.

- Consider choosing unfinished or finished wood décor and furniture pieces (rather than painted) for the resilience area of your home.

- Create a necklace or bracelet of wood beads. Choose an affirmation from earlier in the chapter. As you string each bead, repeat the affirmation once.

VERTICAL STRIPES

The upward/downward movement of vertical stripes and the way they unite below and above evoke trees, forests, rainfall, lightning, and the energy of this key.

Here are some ideas for activating the resilience key with them:

- When appropriate, consider choosing vertically striped prints for the resilience area of the home.

- Wear vertical stripes.

FLORAL OR LEAF PATTERNS AND PRINTS

Naturally, because this key is aligned with healthy plants and trees, floral and leaf patterns and prints invoke the associated energies.

Here are some ways to activate the resilience key with them:

- When appropriate, consider choosing floral or leaf patterns and prints for the resilience area of the home.

- Wear floral or leaf patterns and prints.

COTTON, SISAL, BAMBOO, AND OTHER PLANT–DERIVED MATERIALS

Like wood, plant-derived materials emanate vibrant, upwardly moving energy that is in alignment with this key.

Here are some ways to activate the resilience key with them:

- When appropriate, consider choosing these materials for the resilience area of the home.

- Wear plant-derived fabrics.

Resilience Key Deities

Divinities that are associated with nature, weather, and the earth are especially in alignment with the resilience key. Below you'll find some that fall into these categories. To help activate and heal your relationship with this key, you might strike up a relationship with any or all of them. You might also wear jewelry depicting one of them or display one or more of them in the resilience area of your home or on your altar.

IRIS

The Greek goddess of rainbows, Iris not only shows us the shimmering miracle contained within falling rain, but she provides the connection between heaven and earth, mortals and the Divine. She also supplies the clouds with the water necessary to nourish the earth and her creatures.

GREEN MAN

A beloved Neopagan and ancient European deity, and an incarnation of the universal divine masculine aspect, the Green Man is the leafy green god of vegetation, life, health, and rebirth.

GAIA

Gaia is the ancient Greek primordial Mother Goddess. Many modern Pagans adore her as the Goddess made manifest as the entirety of the earth. Thanks to physicist James Lovelock's Gaia Theory, even modern atheists recognize "Gaia" as an acceptable name for the living, breathing, interconnected organism that comprises planet Earth and all of her inhabitants.

Resilience Key Animals

Like deities, each animal carries its own unique qualities and helpful energy. To activate the resilience key in your life, you can work with the animals below through meditation, prayer, altars, or imagery in your home, on your altar, or on your person (as in jewelry or tattoos).

HERON OR EGRET

According to author and animal totem expert Ted Andrews, herons represent "aggressive self-determination and self-reliance." In other words, they're ready to meet their destiny head-on and to weather the storms of life with courage and aplomb. The way they stand firmly on the earth even as water surges around them is a quintessential image of the resilience key.

KANGAROO

Like deep tree roots holding space and providing nourishment for the newest shoots and leaves, kangaroos keep their offspring close to offer them the foundation they need in order to grow up healthy and strong. Their ability to survive in hot, dry climates also demonstrates their resourceful and resilient nature, and the fact that they only move forward (not backward) symbolizes our necessary forward movement through all our life challenges.

PENGUIN

Talk about banding together to weather a storm! Penguins do it every year and generally demonstrate resilience during every second of their existence as they live their lives in the harshest and coldest of climates.

RAVEN AND CROW

As dark harbingers of mystery, transformation, and the land beyond; hearty scavengers; and demonstrators of close family and family-like relationships, ravens and crows are powerful representations of resilience key energy.

Resilience Key Colors

To activate or enhance the resilience key in your life, you might work with any or all of the following colors, perhaps in one or more of the following ways:

- Wear one or more of them.

- Create a charm incorporating one or more of them, and place it in the resilience area of your home.

- Decorate with one or more of these colors, in any combination, in the resilience area of your home:

  Green: Life, rebirth, the wood element, upward movement.

  Blue: A color associated with both joy and sadness, blue also has upward movement like green but is also aligned with water and the sky.

Teal/Turquoise: A fusion of the two descriptions above (for green and blue), teal is aligned with the immune system and prospering on all levels.

Black: A secondary color for this key, black is associated with deep water, death, rebirth, and the great beyond.

Resilience Key Herbs

CEDAR

Cedar has a very solid, grounding, strengthening energy. Its scent can infuse us with feelings of safety and serenity and can remind us that we are always perfectly supported by the Divine, our loved ones, our ancestors, and the planet.

Try:

- Diffusing the essential oil in your space.

- Misting the space with spring water into which you've added a few drops of cedar essential oil.

- Spending time in quiet contemplation with a cedar tree, hugging a cedar tree, or meditating with your spine against a cedar tree.

- Burning a stick or cone of cedar incense.

- Adding a few drops of cedar essential oil to your bathwater.

DESERT SAGE

With a very sweet, comforting, and spiritually cleansing scent, desert sage smoke can help us feel like we are in the safest, gentlest, most nourishing, most supportive space imaginable.

Try:

- Diffusing smoke from a smoldering bundle of dried desert sage around your space (aka smudging). Be sure to carry a small dish beneath it to catch any burning embers.

EUCALYPTUS

In addition to energizing and clarifying the mind, the scent of eucalyptus literally strengthens the immune system. During times of emotional upheaval, it can soothe, uplift, and lend courage.

Try:

- Diffusing the essential oil in your space.

- Misting the space with spring water into which you've added a few drops of eucalyptus essential oil.

- Bringing eucalyptus leaves into the home.

Resilience Key Crystals

To receive the resilience key–enhancing benefits of any of the crystals below, wear or carry one of them, or place one of them in the resilience area of your home. You may also empower one or both of them with any of the resilience key affirmations from earlier in this chapter.

BLOODSTONE

A deep, luxuriously green stone with blood-red flecks, bloodstone strengthens our health and immunity and cleanses the blood and circulatory system. On the emotional level, it helps heal grief and old family issues while fortifying our courage, resilience, and self-love and encouraging connection with a vibrant social support system.

MOSS AGATE

If ever a stone contained the energy of the lush green earth and the goddess Gaia, it's moss agate. Simply holding a moss agate can give you that nourished, nurtured, grounded, centered, part-of-something-bigger-than-you feeling that you get while standing in a forest.

PHANTOM QUARTZ

Often appearing as a clear quartz containing what appears to be a hologram of another, smaller crystal structure within, phantom quartz helps us gain a healthy perspective on past events and feel strengthened by our own personal and family history. It can also assist us in accessing ancient knowing/genetic memory, ancestral guidance, and wisdom we may have carried over from our past lives.

Resilience Key Master Ritual

If, after reading through this entire book once, you determine that the resilience key is the key that could use the most help in your life right now, performing the following ritual will activate and calibrate this key for you in an ideal way. Or perform this ritual anytime you feel that your resilience key is in need of some major help.

Because the art of bliss is a holistic science, not only will your resilience key benefit from this ritual, but every other life key will benefit as well.

INGREDIENTS

> A juice drink or smoothie made from mainly
>   leafy greens (romaine, kale, spinach,
>   etc.), green vegetables, or sprouts (alfalfa,
>   clover, wheatgrass, etc.), covered
>
> Essential oil of eucalyptus in an oil burner
>
> A stick of cedar incense in a holder
>
> A bundle of dried desert sage
>
> A lighter or matches
>
> 3 healthy houseplants (such as
>   jade, bamboo, or pothos)

At the four cardinal points around an invisible circle approximately six feet in diameter, place the incense holder at the east point and the plants at the other three. Place the oil burner, sage bundle, lighter/matches, and covered juice drink near the incense holder.

Light the incense and oil burner as you say:

> I now summon my spiritual support system.
> I now summon my ancestral support system.
> I now connect with the earth, the trees,
>   the animals, and my human support
>   system in this physical incarnation.

Light the sage bundle and smudge the interior and perimeter of the circle as you say:

> I now clear the way for comfort and strength.
> I now clear the way for the healing
>   of old childhood issues.
> I now clear the way for the
>   healing of past-life issues.
> I now clear the way for vibrant physical health.
> I now clear the way for the joy and pain that are
>   the natural effects of living and loving fully.
> I am safe.
> I am loved.
> I am nourished.
> I am supported.
> I am strong.
> I emerge victoriously because I navigate
>   my challenges with the knowledge that
>   everything is perfectly unfolding.

Extinguish the sage and sit in the center of the circle with your spine straight, facing east. Relax, take some deep breaths, and feel yourself supported on either side and from behind by the plants, your ancestors, your loved ones, your spiritual helpers, and All That Is. When you feel ready, uncover the drink. Hold it in both hands and say:

> As I consume this drink of vibrant green,
>   I nourish my body and fortify my spirit.
> I feel my spirit and life-force energy surging
>   upward toward the sky like a growing tree,
>   and I feel my body being nourished like
>   a fertile field in a gentle rain. I internalize
>   the energy of resilience. On all levels I
>   am strong, healthy, sturdy, harmonious,
>   balanced, courageous, and alive.

Relax and drink.

9 | Synergy

In the center of a storm there is stillness. Inside each molecule there is an incomprehensibly vast stretch of empty space. Were it not for the silence, music would just be noise. Were it not for the blankness, paintings would just be paint. At the foundation of your consciousness, there is a place beyond time, beyond attachment, and beyond the appearance of form. When you are in touch with this place, your perceptions and life conditions arise like sparkling waves and naturally fall into a harmonious and pleasing rhythm, and you feel balanced, blissful, and wise.

**This is the alchemical essence
of life key #9: synergy.**

This life key is a little different than the other eight. Rather than having its own distinct energies and qualities, it's the place where all the other keys merge and mix; you might think of it as the hub of a wheel. Still, if the energies associated with this life key are flowing harmoniously, the following statements will be true for you:

- I feel that all elements of my life are in harmony and balance with one another.

- At the core of my being, I feel safe.

- I sense a stillness and an emptiness that underlie all things.

- A part of me is never in doubt because I know that the truest part of me is eternal and at one with All That Is.

- I feel empowered.

- I feel unified and whole.

- I know that I am the master of my own destiny.

Qualities Associated with the Synergy Key

While the synergy key doesn't possess its own distinct qualities, per se, when it is activated—when all the other keys are able to merge and mix in an ideal way—certain perceptible qualities will arise.

The following descriptions are designed to help you determine how well the synergy key is already flowing in your life, and also to begin creating subtle shifts that will prepare you to more fully activate it.

GENERAL HARMONY AND BALANCE

Because the synergy key allows all areas of our life to merge and mix, general feelings of harmony and balance are a result.

FEELING SAFE

This key also has to do with our core, or the very center of our mental/physical/emotional/spiritual selves. As such, when it's activated and flowing (and especially when all the other areas are also activated and flowing), we feel at home in our bodies and lives: in other words, we feel safe.

AWARENESS OF SPACE CONSCIOUSNESS

In *Stillness Speaks*, author and spiritual teacher Eckhart Tolle writes:

> Stillness is your essential nature. What is stillness? The inner space or awareness in which the words on this page are being perceived and become thoughts. Without that awareness, there would be no perception, no thoughts, no world. You are that awareness, disguised as a person.

When our synergy key is activated and flowing, we are able to hold that awareness so that our life conditions have space around them. That way we can recognize their true nature, let them be what they are, and know that they will eventually fade back to the nothingness from which they came. That knowledge gives us the perspective that we need to thrive and to experience balance in the truest sense of the word.

WHOLENESS

The synergy key also allows us to connect the dots between all aspects of ourselves and our life so that we recognize that we are, even now, complete unto ourselves. Nothing is missing. We are whole.

EMPOWERMENT

With space consciousness, harmony, safety, balance, and a feeling of wholeness, we feel empowered to do and to be whatever our heart of hearts most desires.

Synergy Key-Related Situations

Life situations and intentions that are related to the synergy key include:

- Bringing our lives into balance
- Feeling centered, grounded, and empowered
- Feeling safe
- Effectively mastering our moods and life conditions
- Feeling that we are the masters of our own destiny
- Understanding the interplay of all life keys in order to bring them into harmony in the most ideal of ways

Synergy Key Affirmations

My life is in balance.

Balance and harmony flow through every aspect of my life.

I am whole and complete unto myself.

I am in touch with the vast, empty space within and
around me.

In the center of my being, I am still.

All moments are one moment, and in this moment
I am safe.

The Alchemy of Synergy

Time and again in this book, you've come across the phrase
"the art of bliss is a holistic science." And since the synergy
key is like the hub of a wheel—where all the other keys
meet and interact—you'll notice that this key has fewer cor-
respondences and qualities of its own. You'll also learn some
advanced alchemical secrets as we discuss how each life key
supports and interacts with each other life key.

Synergy Key Symbols

THE NUMBER FIVE

In Chinese cosmology, five elements interact dynamically to make up the entire physical and nonphysical world:
earth, wood, fire, water, and metal. In Wicca and some other
Earth-based religions, the same is true, though the elements
are named and perceived in a slightly different way: earth, air,
fire, water, and ether. Additionally, from our center we extend
outward in five appendages, all of which are distinct and yet
part of the one unified whole: two arms, two legs, and a head.

This pattern is repeated at the end of each arm and each leg in the form of fingers and toes.

In *Sacred Number*, Miranda Lundy writes:

> Five marries male and female—as two and three in some cultures, or three and two in others—and so it is the universal number of reproduction and biological life. It is also the number of water, every molecule of which is the corner of a pentagon…water shows its quality as being [that of] flow, dynamism, and life.

In other words, five is the number of synergistic magical interactions and the alchemical interplay of elements that create our life conditions and all of life as we know it.

Additionally, this area acts as an equalizer of sorts: with five at the center of the magic square, whatever two areas it falls between (horizontally, vertically, or diagonally) must add up together to the solid, balanced number ten.

Here are some ideas for activating the synergy key with the number five:

- String five beads on a piece of hemp twine: one red, one yellow, one white, one black, and one green. Empower by holding it between your palms with your hands in prayer pose and repeating one of the affirmations from earlier in the chapter five times. Wear as a bracelet or necklace or place in the synergy area of your home.

- Fill a water bottle, hold it in both hands, and empower it by repeating one of the affirmations from earlier in this chapter five times. Drink throughout the day. Repeat daily until you feel this key is sufficiently activated.

- Take five drops of Bach Rescue Remedy under the tongue first thing in the morning daily until you feel balanced and whole.

- Take five drops of white chestnut essence under the tongue before bed nightly until the bottle is empty.

PENTAGRAMS

The symbol of harmoniously interacting earth energies and five-element balance in both Taoist and Earth-based cosmologies, each point of a pentagram interacts uniquely and dynamically with each other point through the lines of the star and the points along the circle.

Here are some ways to activate the synergy key with them:

- Place a round rug depicting a pentagram in the synergy area of your home.

- Place a pentagram decoration in the synergy area of your home.

- Wear a piece of jewelry or clothing depicting a pentagram.

- Carve a pentagram into a white, off-white, yellow, or beige candle; empower with one of the affirmations from earlier in

the chapter; place in the synergy area of
your home or on your altar; and light.

YIN/YANG SYMBOL

The yin/yang is the symbol of masculine/feminine balance and the harmonious interplay of the polarities. As such, it can help activate the energies associated with this life key.

Ways to activate the synergy key with it:

- Place a yin/yang decoration in the
  synergy area of your home.

- Place a paper yin/yang symbol on a candle
  holder. Place a white or off-white candle on
  top, empower with one of the affirmations
  from earlier in the chapter, place in the synergy
  area of your home or on your altar, and light.

- Wear a piece of jewelry or clothing
  depicting a yin/yang symbol.

FLAT EXPANSES OF LAND OR EMPTY SPACE

Flat expanses of land or empty space evoke a feeling of expansiveness, grounding, and possibility. In traditional Chinese architecture, the home was often positioned around an open courtyard at the very center of the floor plan (i.e., the synergy area), allowing space for the harmonious interplay of the energies associated with the other eight areas. Today we can call in similarly auspicious energies by employing any or all of the following ideas:

- Keep the center of your floor plan as open and clutter-free as possible.

- Spend time in or near flat expanses of land (perhaps go for a walk or have a picnic in a meadow, grassland, or field).

- Place imagery depicting flat expanses of land in the synergy area of the home.

THE OTHER EIGHT KEYS

Because this is the open space in which all other keys interact, you might like to allow décor, color schemes, etc., from the other eight areas to gently spill over into the central mix. In other words, while it's important to keep it as open and clutter-free as possible, feel free to let the other life keys swirl together naturally in the center of your floor plan. And while you might like to choose décor based on the above recommendations, there's no need to designate space in your home exclusively for synergy key symbols and colors.

In essence, be easy and natural about this area, but do be mindful of clutter and keeping as open a feeling as possible.

Synergy Key Colors

To activate or enhance the synergy key in your life, you might work with any or all of the following colors, perhaps in any of the following ways:

- Decorate with one or more of the colors, in any combination, in the synergy area of your home.

- Choose one or more of them when designing charms and rituals related to activating the synergy key.

- Wear one or more of them with the intention to create the necessary space in your life for balance and harmony to occur.

    Yellow/Buttercream/Goldenrod: The earthy, grounding colors of the harvest, grain fields, the solar plexus chakra, and the Chinese earth element, shades of yellow create that spacious–yet–grounded feeling that is so conducive to harmonious balance.

    Off-White and Beige: The quintessence of neutral, off-white, and beige evokes feelings of clarity and open space.

Synergistic Interactions

4 Prosperity	**9** Radiance	**2** Romance
3 Resilience	**5** Synergy	**7** Creativity
8 Serenity	**1** Life Path	**6** Synchronicity

SUPPORTIVE RELATIONSHIPS

In supportive relationships, one area supports and lends structure to another area.

> **Serenity (8) Supports Romance (2):** Loving and caring for ourselves, spending quiet time alone, and spending alone time in nature all create the necessary emotional conditions for experiencing ideal and harmonious romance.
>
> **Life Path (1) Supports Radiance (9):** When we're in touch with our authenticity and what brings us joy, we are free to radiate it out into the world with integrity and in a way that nourishes and brings blessings to us and to everyone.
>
> **Synchronicity (6) Supports Prosperity (4):** Receiving help from the seen and unseen worlds and being in the right place at the

right time are important prerequisites to
receiving prosperity and experiencing luxury.

Resilience (3) Supports Creativity (7): When
we weather the storms of life, we gain grist for
the creativity mill. When we're resilient, we can
sustain the vulnerability and effort necessary to
successfully express our creativity. And, when
we heal our old childhood, family, and past-life
issues, we give new life and new opportunity
to future generations in our immediate
family and our extended human family.

4 Prosperity	9 Radiance	2 Romance
3 Resilience	5 Synergy	7 Creativity
8 Serenity	1 Life Path	6 Synchronicity

EXPRESSIVE RELATIONSHIPS

In expressive relationships, each supported area (see above) allows the area that supports it to be expressed in a healthy way rather than being dammed up or stagnant.

Romance (2) Expresses Serenity (8):
Nothing helps channel our self-improvement
efforts like connecting with another
human being, and when we experience
the sensual pleasures of life, we come even
more deeply into the present moment.

Radiance (9) Expresses Life Path (1): Once
we align with our true nature, we must share
our gifts with the world so that divine energies
can flow through us freely and in ideal ways.

**Prosperity (4) Expresses Synchronicity
(6):** Connection with the heavenly
realm seeks to be expressed as luxury
and success in the physical realm.

Creativity (7) Expresses Resilience (3):
Our life challenges want to be transmuted
into playful expression so that we can
move through them, learn from them,
and beautify the world in the process.

4 Prosperity	9 Radiance	2 Romance
3 Resilience	5 Synergy	7 Creativity
8 Serenity	1 Life Path	6 Synchronicity

CLEARING RELATIONSHIPS

In clearing relationships, one area creates the space for another area to blossom.

Serenity (8) Clears the Way for Life Path (1): When we are quiet, we can more easily get in touch with our authenticity and our depth.

Life Path (1) Clears the Way for Synchronicity (6): When we know and trust ourselves and know what we're doing and why, those in both seen and unseen realms are more likely to offer assistance.

Synchronicity (6) Clears the Way for Creativity (7): When things flow easily and effortlessly, playfulness and fun naturally arise.

Creativity (7) Clears the Way for Romance (2): Spontaneity and joy help attract and maintain scintillating romantic conditions.

Romance (2) Clears the Way for Radiance (9): Connecting with our senses sparks

our radiant beauty and opens us up
to sharing our light with others.

**Radiance (9) Clears the Way for
Prosperity (4):** Shining our light and
sharing our gifts attract all good things.

**Prosperity (4) Clears the Way for Resilience
(3):** When we feel comfortable and
nourished by life, we are more prepared
to weather any storms that may arise.

**Resilience (3) Clears the Way for Serenity
(8):** Traversing the storms of life and
being supported by our family and loved
ones deepen our self-improvement
efforts and our ability to find stillness.

4 ⟶ Prosperity	**9** ⟶ Radiance	**2** Romance
3 Resilience	**5** Synergy	**7** Creativity
8 ⟵ Serenity	**1** ⟵ Life Path	**6** Synchronicity

ESCALATING RELATIONSHIPS

In escalating relationships, one area provides fuel and momentum for another area.

Resilience (3) Escalates Prosperity (4):
The stronger we are and the more connected and supported we feel, the more abundance we attract.

Prosperity (4) Escalates Radiance (9):
Feeling luxurious and supported fuels our confidence and passionate self-expression.

Radiance (9) Escalates Romance (2):
Passion and fire fan the flames of romance.

Romance (2) Escalates Creativity (7): Sensual connection and deep connections with others engender playfulness and childlike wonder.

Creativity (7) Escalates Synchronicity (6):
Openness to possibilities and thinking outside the box opens us up to divine help and miraculous happenings.

Synchronicity (6) Escalates Life Path
(1): Falling into step with divine
intervention offers the guidance and
support we need to strengthen our
alignment with our authentic life path.

Life Path (1) Escalates Serenity (8): When
we know who we are and what brings
us joy, we know what we want to study
and what types of self-improvement
projects we want to embark upon.

Serenity (8) Escalates Resilience (3):
Inner stillness and self-love give us the
strength we need to stay strong and
move flexibly with the flow of life.

The Effect of Each Key on Each Other Key:

The serenity key lends stillness and
clarity to every other key.

The life path key lends meaning and
direction to every other key.

The synchronicity key lends ease and
harmony to every other key.

The creativity key lends playfulness
and joy to every other key.

The romance key lends sensuality and
receptivity to every other key.

The **radiance key** lends energy and success to every other key.

The **prosperity key** lends luxury and comfort to every other key.

The **resilience key** lends support and deep healing to every other key.

Synergy Key Master Ritual

If, after reading through this entire book once, you determine that all the other areas are activated and flowing but just need to interact and connect with each other in a more ideal way, this would be the ritual to perform.

Or perform this ritual if you feel that activating the synergy key at this time is an important step toward clearing the way and establishing the ideal conditions for the successful activation of any or all of the other keys.

INGREDIENTS

A faceted crystal globe (aka "feng shui crystal"), 20–40 mm (about the size of a quarter or silver dollar)

A cone of cinnamon/cinnabar incense and holder

White chestnut essence

Clary sage essential oil

A mister of spring water

As suggested at the beginning of the book, clear all the clutter out of your home that you possibly can. Take all the time you need with this, even if you have to continue this process for a number of days or even weeks. Throw out, donate, sell, or give away the old items, or do whatever you need to do to get rid of them in a way that feels right to you. While you are doing this, be sure to drink at least half your body weight in ounces of water per day.

When this is complete, add 25 drops of clary sage essential oil and 5 drops of white chestnut essence to the mister of spring water. Close the lid and shake. Hold it in both hands and visualize very bright white light coming down through the crown of your head and into your heart, down your arms, out through your hands, and into the bottle. Say:

> I now empower this potion with
>   the energy of harmony.
> I now empower this potion with
>   the energy of balance.
> I am safe, I am powerful, and all is well.

Light the incense cone and place near the center of your floor plan.

Attach the crystal globe to the ceiling in the very center of your floor plan (or as close to the center as possible). Stand beneath it and a little bit to the side of the crystal (so that you can easily see it when you gaze upwards). Hold your hands in prayer pose, close your eyes, take some deep breaths, and relax. Visualize flat, open space extending out in all directions from the crystal. Feel clarity, expansiveness, and possibility

286

emanating from this open space. Know that you are creating the perfect space for the energies of all the other eight keys to perfectly merge and mix. Five times in a row, repeat the following words:

Balanced, blissful synergy is now established in my body, mind, spirit, home, and life.

Now open your eyes, open your palms, direct them upwards toward the crystal, and send the energy of the intention toward the crystal.

When this feels complete, mist the entire space with the potion.

To seal in the energy of the ritual, stand near the crystal once more. Place your hands over your heart and say:

Thank you, thank you, thank you. Blessed be. And so it is.

Allow the incense to continue to burn until it goes out naturally.

Epilogue

This book wanted to be born, and now that it has been, I can feel that it is grateful, just as I am grateful for the experience of giving birth to it. Although I've been familiar with the teachings it contains for quite some time, as I wrote each chapter, new insights appeared within me and presented themselves obviously in the physical world all around me. It was as if the universe was dictating to me—not simply by telling me what to type but through the symbols, dreams, everyday happenings, and kaleidoscopic unfoldings that graced my awareness and everyday perceptions. In the process, my life shifted and expanded to meet my new insights, and (after moving through considerable growing pains along the way) I gained access to even deeper levels of joy, self-love, freedom, clarity, and inspiration than ever before. As you work with the ideas in each chapter, don't be surprised if something similar happens to you.

What's endlessly interesting to me, and what I'm sure you'll discover firsthand, is that the alchemical language in the preceding pages is not static, nor is it exclusive to any one culture, tradition, or faith. Like DNA, it's contained within us, and while it may adhere to certain finite rules, it appears in infinitely shifting patterns that lay the groundwork for infinite variations on the themes of life and human existence.

It's my wish that you have as much fun with the information in this book as I do, and that it will enhance your life in similarly deep and beautiful ways.

Appendix

If one or more of the nine life areas is "missing" from or lies outside of the boundary of your floor plan, there are a number of things you can do to include these energies in your home and life, ranging from very involved to very simple. We'll start with the more involved suggestions and go toward the ones that anyone can do with any space, no matter what. Read through them and find one or more that works for your unique space, feels doable, and resonates as something that will be powerful for you. I suggest reading the book in its entirety before proceeding, or at least being familiar with the area of concern.

A: Fill In with a Room or a Deck

If you have freedom with the area, and you have the funds or skill, you might like to fill in the "missing" floor plan area by adding a room or a deck. The following suggestions are designed to give you some ideas but are not hard and fast

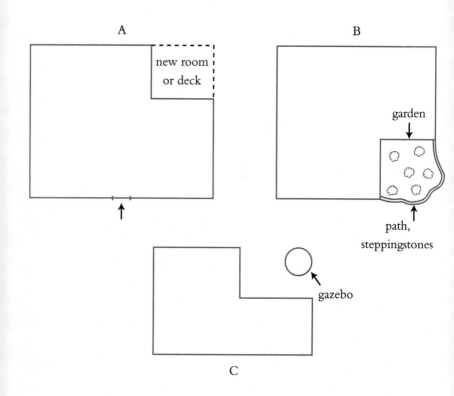

rules. For example, if you have been wanting or needing a specific type of room or deck area, and it'll fit appropriately in the missing area, that would obviously take precedence.

- If it's the serenity area, you might like to add a meditation room, study, exercise room, or meditative deck area.

- If it's the life path area, you might like to add an office, entry, den, or deck with fountain.

- If it's the synchronicity area, you might like to add an office, entry, guest room, exercise room, or sun deck.

- If it's the creativity area, you might like to add an art room, dance studio, child's room, play room, or deck with whimsical ornaments and wind dancers.

- If it's the romance area, you might like to add a master bedroom, cozy den for two, or a deck with a romantic, candlelit dinner feeling.

- If it's the radiance area, you might like to add a kitchen, dining area, dressing room or boudoir, family room, dance studio, or deck with red flowers, fire pit, BBQ, or light catchers.

- If it's the prosperity area, you might like to add a spa-like relaxation room, a family or living room, a den, an office, or a deck with lush plants, wind catchers, chimes, a hot tub, or a fountain.

- If it's the resilience area, you might like to
  add a kitchen, dining room, living room,
  family room, exercise room, or a deck with
  lots of healthy plants and possibly a fountain.

B: Fill In with a Garden

Perhaps you'd like to complete the space energetically by adding a garden and enclosing it along the delineation of the bagua with steppingstones or a path. If you choose to go this route, here are some loose guidelines:

- If it's the serenity area, go for a
  meditative feel in the garden.

- If it's the life path area, you might
  choose black river rocks or add a
  fountain, bird bath, or koi pond.

- If it's the synchronicity area, you might
  choose angelic flowers such as Asian
  lilies and roses or add angel statues or
  statues of other helpful beings.

- If it's the creativity area, go for a
  feeling of fun and whimsy.

- If it's the romance area, you might create a
  romantic/sensual feeling, possibly with roses,
  hibiscus, jasmine, geranium, basil, or other
  fragrant flowers and herbs. Consider a porch
  swing for two or another romantic addition.

- If it's the radiance area, red, pink, or orange blooms would be ideal, as would a fire pit.

- If it's the prosperity area, you might choose purple, red, or blue blossoms; lush-feeling plants such as ferns, palms, or jade; luxurious seating; a water feature like a bird bath, fountain, or pond; or wealth-drawing herbs such as basil and mint.

- If it's the resilience area, lush, healthy, hearty greenery like bamboo, jade, and trees would be ideal, and you might consider adding a small water feature.

C: Complete the Space with a Substantial Yard Addition

To go a simpler (but no less effective) route, you might like to complete the space by adding a substantial yard addition at the corner of the formerly "missing" space. For example:

- If it's the serenity area, you might add a meditating Buddha or Quan Yin statue, large rock, tree, lamppost, or fountain.

- If it's the synchronicity area, you might add an angel statue, lamppost, large rock, or tree.

- If it's the romance area, you might add a statue of Krishna and Radha, a porch swing for two, a gazebo, two trees side by side (but not so close that they will hamper each other's growth), or two lampposts side by side.

- If it's the prosperity area, you might add a statue of Maitreya (laughing Buddha), freestanding wind chimes, a lamppost, a fountain, or a tree.

(Since this cure takes place at the corners, the other areas are not applicable.)

D: Complete the Space with a Crystal

If all of this is a little too involved, or if none of the above suggestions are possible for whatever reason, you might consider burying a white quartz crystal point (or two if it's the romance area), point-side up and very slightly angling toward the center of the floor plan, at the corner of the formerly missing area. Choose a crystal that is at least four inches long and feels somewhat substantial. Cleanse it first by running it under cold water for two minutes, setting it in sunlight for at least ten minutes, and burning white sage smoke around it. Then, before placing it in the earth, hold it in both hands and charge it with the intention to symbolically complete the space and bring in the energies of the formerly missing area. You might send intentions and positive feelings related to this life area at this time as well.

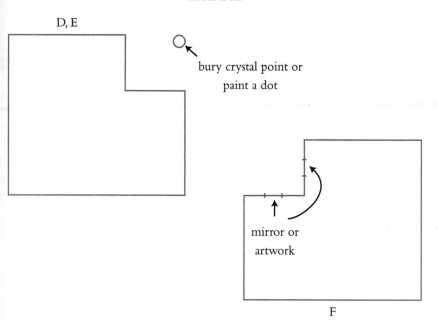

D, E

bury crystal point or
paint a dot

mirror or
artwork

F

E: Complete the Space with a Dot

Sometimes you can't do any of the above suggestions because the corner of the missing area happens to fall on your driveway or another paved area. If this is the case, if it feels right to you and if you have the freedom to do so, you might like to complete the space by painting a dot between the size of a quarter and a silver dollar on the pavement. A round, bright red dot would be the classic choice, but if you want to get specific, consider the following ideas:

- If it's the serenity area, paint a green,
  blue, or black circle or square.

- If it's the synchronicity area, paint a black circle.

- If it's the romance area, paint a red heart or two red hearts side by side.

- If it's the prosperity area, paint a red, green, or purple circle.

F: Create the Illusion of Space with a Mirror or Artwork

Perhaps you can't exactly perform any of the above suggestions because you live in an apartment, the outdoor space belongs to someone else, or for some other reason entirely. If so, you might like to bring in the energies associated with the missing area by creating the illusion of space. To do this, hang a mirror or art with depth (such as a house with a long stretch of field behind it, or an ocean vista) on the wall bordering the missing area. That way, when you look toward the area, you will feel as if there is space there. Simply choosing and placing these items will help solidify your intention to bring in these energies.

If you choose art with depth, choose artwork that gives you positive feelings related to the life area that you're intending to include.

G: Emphasize the Area in the Floor Plan of One or More Rooms

You may be surprised to learn that each room has its own floor plan within the floor plan. In other words, your home isn't the only place with a prosperity area: your living room, bathroom, bedroom, etc., each have one as well. While it's not necessary to concentrate on this too much when working with the décor of your home or with the alchemy of bliss in general, it can come in handy when you want to compensate for having a certain area outside of your floor plan.

To discover the magical floor plan of a room, determine the main door to the room. If there is more than one door and you're not sure which is the "main" door, you can discover this by determining which one is closer to the front door or which one borders on one of the main tributaries of the home. Once you've determined the main door to the room, simply consider this the front door, draw an imaginary tick-tack-toe board over the space (just as you did in the introduction with the entirety of your floor plan), and determine which area is which.

To illustrate how you would then utilize this information, let's imagine the prosperity area is the area that is "missing" from your home's floor plan. To balance this condition, you might obtain a silver dollar for each room in your home, cleanse the silver dollars in salt water, empower them in the sun and then in the light of the full moon, and place one in the prosperity area of each room. As you do so, you might repeat one of the affirmations from the end of chapter 7 four times.

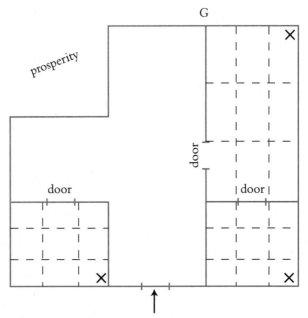

The Xs mark where prosperity
charms should be placed.

Bibliography

Andrews, Ted. *Animal-speak*. Woodbury, MN: Llewellyn, 1993.

Blake, William. "Auguries of Innocence." *The Complete Poetry and Prose of William Blake*. Ed. David V. Erdman. Berkeley, CA: University of California Press, 1965.

Bradley, Marion Zimmer. *The Mists of Avalon*. New York: Ballantine, 1987.

Cameron, Julia. *The Artist's Way: A Spiritual Path to Higher Creativity*. New York: Tarcher, 1992.

———. *The Vein of Gold: A Journey to Your Creative Heart*. New York: Tarcher, 1996.

Carroll, Lewis. *Alice in Wonderland*. New York: Macmillan, 1897.

Collins, Terah Kathryn. *The Western Guide to Feng Shui*. Carlsbad, CA: Hay House, 1996.

———. *The Western Guide to Feng Shui: Room by Room*. Carlsbad, CA: Hay House, 1999.

Cunningham, Scott. *Cunningham's Encyclopedia of Magical Herbs*. St. Paul, MN: Llewellyn, 1985.

———. *Magical Aromatherapy: The Power of Scent*. St. Paul, MN: Llewellyn, 1989.

Deida, David. *Dear Lover: A Woman's Guide to Men, Sex, and Love's Deepest Bliss*. Louisville, CO: Sounds True, 2006.

Gladwell, Malcolm. *Outliers: The Story of Success*. New York: Little, Brown, and Company: 2008.

Greene, Liz, and Juliet Sharman-Burke. *The Mythic Tarot*. New York: Fireside, 1986.

Hanh, Thich Nhat. *Old Path White Clouds: Walking in the Footsteps of the Buddha*. Berkeley, CA: Parallax Press, 1991.

Hesse, Hermann. *Magister Ludi (The Glass Bead Game)*. Zurich: Fretz & Wasmuth Verlag AG, 1943.

Illes, Judika. *The Element Encyclopedia of 5000 Spells*. London: HarperElement, 2004.

———. *The Element Encyclopedia of Witchcraft*. London: HarperElement, 2005.

———. *The Encyclopedia of Spirits: The Ultimate Guide to the Magic of Fairies, Genies, Demons, Ghosts, Gods, and Goddesses*. New York: HarperOne, 2009.

Jung, Carl. *Synchronicity: An Acausal Connecting Principle*. Princeton, NJ: Princeton University Press, 1952.

Katie, Byron. *Loving What Is: Four Questions That Can Change Your Life*. New York: Three Rivers Press, 2003.

Kennedy, David Daniel. *Feng Shui for Dummies*. Hoboken, NJ: Wiley Publishing, 2001.

Kingston, Karen. *Clear Your Clutter with Feng Shui*. New York: Broadway Books, 1998.

Linn, Denise. *Past Lives, Present Miracles*. Carlsbad, CA: Hay House, 2008.

Lundy, Miranda. *Sacred Geometry*. New York: Walker & Company, 2001.

————. *Sacred Number: The Secret Qualities of Quantities*. New York: Walker & Company, 2005.

Lurker, Manfred. *The Routledge Dictionary of Gods, Goddesses, Devils, and Demons*. London: Routledge, 1987.

Medici, Marina. *Good Magic*. New York: Fireside, 1988.

Melody. *Love Is in the Earth*. Wheat Ridge, CO: Earth-Love Publishing House, 1995.

Nietzsche, Friedrich. *The Portable Nietzsche*. New York: Penguin, 1977.

New Advent. "St. Christopher." *Catholic Encyclopedia*. http://www.newadvent.org/cathen/03728a.htm

Ojedele, Olokuntogun Ifasehun. "Who Is the Orisa Called Olokun?" *Roots and Rooted: For Those That*

Love Traditional African Religion. Roots and Rooted, 8 May 2008. http://www.rootsandrooted.org/

Penczak, Christopher. "Gay Gods." *Gay Paganism: A Celebration*. Witchvox, 26 October 2001. http://www.witchvox.com/

Rose, Carol. *Spirits, Fairies, Leprechauns, and Goblins: An Encyclopedia*. New York: Norton, 1996.

Rosenberg, Marshall B. *Nonviolent Communication: A Language of Life*. Encinitas, CA: Puddle Dancer Press, 2003.

Sendak, Maurice. *Where the Wild Things Are*. London: Puffin, 1970.

Spitzer, K. D. "Magic Squares." *Llewellyn's 2009 Magical Almanac*. Woodbury, MN: Llewellyn, 2008.

Tolle, Eckhart. *A New Earth: Awakening to Your Life's Purpose*. New York: Plume, 2006.

———. *Stillness Speaks*. Novato, CA: New World Library, 2003.

Virtue, Doreen. *Archangels and Ascended Masters*. Carlsbad, CA: Hay House, 2003.

———. *Goddess Guidance Oracle Cards*. Carlsbad, CA: Hay House, 2004.

Virtue, Doreen, and Lynnette Brown. *Angel Numbers*. Carlsbad, CA: Hay House, 2005.

Whitehurst, Tess. *The Good Energy Book: Creating Harmony and Balance for Yourself and Your Home.* Woodbury, MN: Llewellyn, 2012.

————. *Magical Clutter Clearing Boot Camp* (Kindle Edition). Los Angeles: Chapel House, 2011.

————. *Magical Housekeeping: Simple Charms and Practical Tips for Creating a Harmonious Home.* Woodbury, MN: Llewellyn, 2010.

Yun, Venerable Master Hsing. *Sutra of the Medicine Buddha with an Introduction, Comments, and Prayers.* Hacienda Heights, CA: Buddha's Light Publishing, 2002.

To Write to the Author

If you wish to contact the author or would like more information about this book, please write to the author in care of Llewellyn Worldwide and we will forward your request. Both the author and the publisher appreciate hearing from you and learning of your enjoyment of this book and how it has helped you. Llewellyn Worldwide cannot guarantee that every letter written to the author can be answered, but all will be forwarded. Please write to:

Tess Whitehurst
℅ Llewellyn Worldwide
2143 Wooddale Drive
Woodbury, MN 55125-2989

Please enclose a self-addressed stamped envelope for reply
or $1.00 to cover costs. If outside the USA, enclose an
international postal reply coupon.

Many of Llewellyn's authors have websites with additional information and resources. For more information, please visit our website:

WWW.LLEWELLYN.COM